I0569576

GOOD NEWS FOR A FRACTURED SOCIETY

MATTHEW SPEAKS TO DIVISIONS OF POWER, WEALTH, GENDER, AND RELIGIOUS PLURALISM

STEPHEN McCUTCHAN

PRIMIX
PUBLISHING
THE WRITE CHOICE

Primix Publishing
11620 Wilshire Blvd
Suite 900, West Wilshire Center, Los Angeles, CA, 90025
www.primixpublishing.com
Phone: 1-800-538-5788

Published by Primix Publishing: 02/21/2024

ISBN: 979-8-89194-060-4(sc)
ISBN: 979-8-89194-061-1(e)

Library of Congress Control Number: 2024901316

To my wife, Sandy, whose editorial work
should merit the title of co-author

CONTENTS

INTRODUCTION

Given the ideologically divided, tension filled world in which we live, imagine hearing someone tell you how God can work through these divisions in a way that offers hope and healing for the world. I believe that this is exactly what Matthew seeks to do in his gospel. This book describes Matthew's inspired vision for our world. In essence, it fleshes out what Paul meant when he said, "In Christ God was reconciling the world to himself, not counting their trespasses against them, and entrusting the message of reconciliation to us (2 Corinthians 5:19).

The Hebrew Scriptures tell the story of how God chose to accomplish a divine work of reconciliation through a chosen people who demonstrated the same strengths and weaknesses as most people in the world today. Matthew interpreted the life, death, and resurrection of Jesus as the midrash, or commentary on the Hebrew Scriptures, that revealed how God worked with both the shadow side and the bright side of human nature to accomplish the divine purpose.

The contemporary church, in a similar manner to Matthew's congregation, must determine the church's response to a world divided between the powerful and the powerless (chapter 1), the Christian faith and other faiths (chapter 2), male and female (chapter 3), and the wealthy and the poor (chapter 4). Following an interpretation of how Matthew found hope in the face of such divisions, the fifth chapter recognizes that most contemporary churches feel helpless in the face of such overwhelming realities. The author then describes Matthew's understanding of how God works through resistance and even betrayal to transform the world. The final chapter explores God's intention to bring about a common witness of Jews and Christians in the reconciliation of the entire world. Matthew's Gospel provides a vision of hope that enables today's Christians to respond with strength to the challenges of the world and have confidence that their efforts are not in vain.

In the midst of a tumultuous world, Matthew proclaimed a gospel based on the assumption that God had not lost control of history but was intimately involved in its development. For Christians, the central revelation of God's involvement is in the person of Jesus whom we acclaim as the Christ of God. This Jesus, whom we know through the scriptural witness of his life, was not only an historical figure in time but also is a continuing presence that seeks the reconciliation of God's creation to God's purpose.

God, through Christ, established the church as Christ's body through which Christ's continuing presence can be experienced. Through the church, with all its foibles and weaknesses, God continues to demonstrate the promise of reconciliation for God's creation. In the church, God works with both the shadow side and the bright side of the creation to reconcile it to God's purpose. In doing so, God does not override our freedom but includes it in the working out of the divine purpose.

This leads to the conviction that the church is more than a religious organization. The church is the Body of Christ and the instrument by which God addresses the faithful. The Scripture, in this case the Gospel of Matthew, is a means by which God can call God's people to faithfulness in the church.

This examination of Matthew emphasizes the corporate nature of the church. The issue for Matthew was how the life and ministry of Christ revealed God's intention for Christ's body, the church. In contrast to the current consumer mentality of asking what the church must do to attract new members, Matthew raised the questions of what we must do to be obedient to God and how we can do that in a manner that is loving towards our neighbor.

A particular emphasis for Matthew was the consistent nature of God's unfolding revelation as seen in the way in which the life of Christ fulfilled that which was spoken of in the Hebrew Scriptures. The pattern of Jesus' life embodied in one person the life of Israel. For example, like Israel Jesus was affirmed as God's only child. In a similar manner to Israel, Jesus went into Egypt in order to ensure his survival. Like Israel Jesus had his wilderness experience in which he was tempted and had to decide whether he would trust God for his survival. The twelve disciples reflected a similar pattern to the twelve tribes of Israel. This will be examined further in the final chapter.

The question for the early church was what would it mean for Israel or the church if it were totally obedient to God in a world that did not honor such obedience? Both Israel and the church struggled with whether faithfulness was possible in a world that did not honor God. The fear was that in being obedient to God their very survival was put at risk. The disturbing response in the Gospels was that such fears had merit. Jesus, the obedient one, was crucified. But the Gospels further proclaimed that God, not death, had the final word. The continuing question for the church, which continually wrestles with the issue of survival, is whether it can trust such a truth.

The words of Scripture were shaped by the language, culture, and time period in which they were written; yet when that is understood, they can also speak freshly to each new age and communicate through new languages and cultures. While God can address humans through many sources, the Scriptures are God's gift to the church through which God can speak to us as a community of faith.

The intent of this study is to engage you in a conversation with God as to the meaning of your life as you share in the living Body of Christ. The study approaches Scripture from a "figural" perspective that suggests that the pattern of Christ's life, which reflected the patterns of the life of Israel, reveals the pattern for the church in our day and time. My hope is that this study will challenge the church to reflect on the nature of the church and the manner in which we can listen to the spirit of God addressing us. It is based on the assumption that the Word of God has been "incarnated" or fleshed out in time–first in creation, more specifically in the life of Israel, most concretely in the life of Jesus, and continually in the life of the church.

A guide to studying this book is contained in the text itself. You will find section headings that will set the context for your study. For example, in chapter 1 the first few sections are titled "Claiming One's Rights," "Identifying with the Struggle," "Temptation as Preparation," etc. These section heads give you a sense of the flow of the presentation. If you are teaching a group, it would be good to make a list of the section heads on a separate sheet of paper.

You will also find a series of grayed sentences throughout the text that pose contemporary questions that the author believes Matthew is addressing. These statements should be tested out with the group. Can they give examples from their lives or from today's society that either affirms or denies the assertion being made? If the statement is true, what are the challenges raised for believers. After several people have made their comments, have the group review the biblical example from Matthew and discuss it in light of the previous conversation. If you will keep track of the grayed sections as you discuss them, you will see how the author believes that Matthew is building his understanding of Christ's challenge of our view the world.

A word needs to be said about my approach to Matthew and the society that Matthew addressed. Matthew's Gospel was written in what sociologists call an agrarian society. Several of the divisions that continue to exist in our society existed in a very pronounced form in Matthew's society. For example, the division between the governing elite and the peasantry was so complete that there was almost no communication between them. The governing class saw its position not in public service for the good of the whole society but as a position by which the members could enrich themselves. Government offices were bought and sold like property and even passed down from one generation to another as a form of inheritance. It never would have occurred to members of this ruling class that they had any responsibility for the welfare of the peasantry. Since they saw all forms of work as degrading, they looked upon the peasant class as subhuman and existing only to support the upper classes. So when Jesus suggested that members of the kingdom should voluntarily become the slaves or servants of each other, it was far more radical than just suggesting that people should think of others first. It was a challenge to the very structure that held society together.

The merchant class stood between the ruling elite and the peasantry. Although some were extremely wealthy, because they worked for their wealth and were often in contact with both peasantry and foreigners, they were rarely treated as equals by the ruling class. Yet because the governing class both wanted the goods that they sold and envied their wealth, there was frequent interaction between the elite and the urban merchants. The merchant class feared, resented, and envied the ruling class. Despite the merchants' often negative feelings, when given the opportunity, they often emulated the governing class and sought to be accepted by them. This is an important group to understand because I believe that Herman C. Waetjen[i] makes a persuasive case for the urban setting of Matthew's Gospel and the fact that Matthew's congregation may have consisted of a relatively wealthy urban class of merchants and landowners.

This relatively wealthy, but never fully accepted, urban merchant class was on the one hand not as rigidly traditional as the aristocracy of their society, but at the same time, its members were tempted to emulate the aristocracy in order to gain acceptance that might come about because of their wealth. In their flexibility, they served as possible bridges across divisions within their society, but in the process, they were tempted to reinforce those divisions in order to secure their own positions. In hearing Matthew address them, we hear the gospel addressed to us, who are torn between using our wealth to secure our place in society versus using our wealth to help the less fortunate.

The agrarian society in which Jesus lived was more rigidly patriarchal than ours is today. This was especially true among the upper class who could afford the luxury of relegating women to a position of adornment. The fact that Matthew used so many feminine images in the proclamation of his gospel, given the rigid male dominated society from which he wrote, not only is a challenge to our current understanding of male/female relationships, but these images are a witness to the power of transformation which Matthew experienced in Jesus. In the Gospel of Matthew, we are not reading about some reforms that might make us a better society, but rather we are being confronted by the Christ who challenges us to be transformed and to recognize the signs of the New Creation which even now are entering our world.

In offering these reflections, I would like to give special thanks to the three churches that have shaped my understanding of the Body of Christ as they have shared in ministry with me. They are Bradley Hills Presbyterian Church in Bethesda, Maryland; First Presbyterian Church in Wellsboro, Pennsylvania; and Highland Presbyterian Church in Winston-Salem, North Carolina. I would also like to thank Sharon Pennypacker who typed the first manuscript of this book many years ago as well as my wife, Sandy, and my daughters, Sonia and Nicole, who supported me in the many struggles of ministry and kept me sane when the stresses were high as well as rejoiced with me in the many moments of joy.

CHAPTER 1

RESPONSE TO A WORLD DIVIDED INTO THE POWERFUL AND THE POWERLESS

There is probably no greater issue that confronts our world than the relationship between the powerful and the powerless. Whether we are talking about nations or individuals, the tension created by the disparity between those who have power and those who do not threatens to erupt in a violence that destroys.

Matthew also lived in a society that was fractured by the various power games that were played to achieve status and security. He wrote to a congregation of upper class urban merchants and landlords in an agrarian society who were used to the possession of and striving for power. Yet Matthew proclaimed the Gospel of Jesus of Nazareth, the one who revealed God at work in the world, in a manner contrasted that sharply with the normal approach to power in this world and offered hope for a fractured society.

1

Claiming One's Rights

Matthew's congregation, and we, are urged not to be so quick in exercising judgment on the powerless. To do so may risk missing the creative word that God is revealing in the very experience that offends us.

Because Matthew's people possessed power and used it in relation to those who were less powerful, it is significant that Matthew, unlike Luke, told of the birth of Jesus from Joseph's point of view (1:18-25). As will be indicated in Chapter 3, in this patriarchal society, Mary's betrothal to Joseph meant that she was bound like property to him. The betrothal could be dissolved only if Joseph gave Mary a writ of divorce and not vice-versa. When Mary was found to be with child, Joseph would have been well within his rights to have her stoned to death. The question is how are Christians, who have power, to respond to those who have apparently wronged and offended them?

Joseph saw "doing right" as a communal, rather than an individual issue. It was not, for him, just a case of claiming or defending his rights, but of considering the effect of such a claim on the very person who had offended him. However, Joseph paused to consider the effect of claiming his rights on the other person, Mary. "...Joseph, being a righteous man and unwilling to expose her to public disgrace, planned to dismiss her quietly." He had every reason to believe that she had wronged him, yet he was open to God's revealing how the same event looked from the divine perspective. Too often we are so focused on defending our rights that we do not make space to hear what God would say to us.   "...But just when he had resolved to do this, an angel of the Lord appeared to him..." That spiritual messenger called on Joseph not to claim his "rights," that exercise of vested privilege and authority which no matter how sensitively handled still protects our position in the world, but rather to trust that the spirit of God was working through the very event that seemed so offensive to him.

Joseph was urged to risk identifying with a person who by "rights" was rejected. He was called upon to recognize that the very action which seemed to have violated his "rights" might well contain birth pangs of the Word of God. To have dismissed Mary as an immoral woman, no matter how sensitively handled, would have block ed the possibility of hearing God's word as expressed through Mary and her child.

Identifying with the Struggle

Even for the most sensitive of those who hold power, the usual assumption is that power indicates superiority and by our insightful use of power we can raise the powerless to enjoy the same benefits of life that we do.

In 3:13-17, Jesus came from Galilee to be baptized by John in the Jordan River. John was offering a baptism of repentance. Those who came were to confess that their life had been distorted by the power of sin and to admit the need to turn their life around. In contrast to other religious leaders that Matthew would describe, Jesus displayed no need to project a position of superiority but rather openly presented himself for a baptism of repentance. In doing so, he identified with those who struggle against the powers that oppress them. John, recognizing who Jesus was and therefore seeing no fault in him, objected to baptizing Jesus. But Jesus, in the true prophetic and priestly mode depicted by Moses in Exodus 32:11-14, identified with the struggle of the people. He did not deny John's recognition of his lack of sin, or separation from God, but rather suggested that righteousness is fulfilled not when we have risen above others in our purity but when we have identified with others in their struggle against the powers which leave them in alienation.

MATTHEW SAW GOD IDENTIFYING WITH JESUS WHEN JESUS IDENTIFIED WITH THE PEOPLE WHO WERE STRUGGLING TO ESCAPE THE POWERS THAT DISTORTED THEIR LIVES.

It was when Jesus identified with and participated in the struggle of people to turn their life around (repentance)

3

that Jesus was confirmed by the presence of the Holy Spirit. Matthew saw God identifying with Jesus when Jesus identified with the people who were struggling to escape the powers that distorted their lives. Just as God had heard the groanings of the people of Israel when they were slaves in Egypt (Exodus 2:24--25) and identified with them (Exodus 4:22), when Jesus heard the groanings of the people and identified with them, God confirmed Jesus. The Gospel promises that when we, as the Body of Christ, identify with the genuine struggle of the people, God will confirm us as God's children (John 1:12-13).

Temptation as Preparation

When we do identify with the struggle of the people, it is tempting to believe that we are the saviors of the world.

For Jesus, it was at this high moment in his life when God had confirmed Jesus as God's son and Jesus had received the Spirit or blessing and power of God to carry out God's ministry, that Jesus was tempted by evil (4:1-11). It was that very same spirit of God who had confirmed Jesus who now led Jesus into the wilderness to be tempted by the devil. Satan, which in Hebrew means the adversary, became the servant of God to prepare Jesus for ministry.

The blessing and power of God that enables one to do good and the temptation to do evil are not opposites but often are a necessary part of the same experience. It is in facing that evil rather than seeking to avoid it that we are prepared for ministry.

For those who are accustomed to some of the benefits of power in this world, one of the greatest temptations is to want to serve the needy without risking one's position of comfort in this world.

Jesus is described as deliberately making himself vulnerable. Jesus "fasted forty days and forty nights, and afterwards he was famished." Forty is a biblical symbol for a complete period of time. As God used the forty years of wandering in the wilderness, and the people's experience of complete vulnerability and dependence on God during that time, to prepare the people of Israel to be God's people (Deuteronomy 8:2-4), so now Jesus placed himself in that same state of vulnerability and dependence on God in order to prepare himself for ministry.

Matthew, unlike Mark and Luke, adds the phrase "forty nights" to the forty days, which would immediately suggest comparison with Moses and Elijah. Moses twice spent forty days and forty nights on Mount Sinai. The first time he had been fed by God before the experience (Exodus 24:11,18), and the second time he neither "ate bread nor drank water" (Exodus 34:28). Elijah was fed by God in preparation for a journey of forty days and forty nights into the wilderness (I Kings 19:8). Though God was with Moses during this time and Elijah met God at the end of this period, Jesus, having prepared to meet God, met temptation instead. It was only by experiencing the temptation of power and the fear of the loss of it that Jesus, and later the Body of Christ seen in Matthew's congregation, could be prepared to serve God. For Christians who enjoyed the benefits of affluence, as did members of Matthew's congregation, it must have seemed unnatural to deliberately make oneself vulnerable to temptation. By Jesus' experience, Matthew made clear that for those blessed by God in this life, it is only by facing the temptation of those blessings that we are prepared to serve God.

We often fear temptation will come at the point where we are weakest, but Jesus' experience revealed that it can come at the point of our strength as well.

Having made himself vulnerable in order to be cleansed of all false dependencies and to completely rely upon God, Jesus' very confirmation

BY JESUS' EXPERIENCE, MATTHEW MADE CLEAR THAT FOR THOSE BLESSED BY GOD IN THIS LIFE, IT IS ONLY BY FACING THE TEMPTATION OF THOSE BLESSINGS THAT WE ARE PREPARED TO SERVE GOD.

as the Son of God, "if you are the Son of God..." became the point of temptation.

The first temptation of ministry is to use the blessings of God in response to the needs of humanity in order to confirm one's status as favored by God.

The fact that the first temptation was in the plural, "command these stones to become loaves of bread," would suggest that the temptation was to demonstrate Jesus superiority to Moses and Elijah. They were fed from heaven, but Jesus would be the source of the bread. Jesus could give proof to his divine sonship by being the source of bread for the hungry as God had once been the source of manna in the wilderness (Deuteronomy 8: 3). John 6:30-34 describes this same temptation but in a different context.

That this temptation has larger economic implications for the church as it seeks to respond to the hungry of the world is confirmed by Jesus' response: "One does not live by bread alone, but by every word that comes from the mouth of God." This quotation comes from Deuteronomy 8:3 and was addressed to the whole covenant people. All the people of faith must learn that there is more to life than just using the blessings of God to secure one's economic survival. Where as Israel, in the Hebrew Scriptures, was the Son of God (Exodus 4:22), Matthew saw in Jesus' life a reliving of the experience of Israel. As the Son of God, the temptation was not only to manipulate the gift of divine favor into self-controlled security but also to display one's divinity by becoming the source of bread for the world. Matthew will later describe Jesus as feeding the hungry and responding to human need. These displays of God's power, however, will be in order to set people free and not to manipulate or control them for the purpose of enhancing one's status. And so it should be for the congregation of faith.

The second temptation of ministry is to claim God's protection as a "right" in return for one's faithfulness, to use faith to protect oneself rather than for serving others.

The second temptation for Jesus was to be revered not for what he could produce but for what he had access to. Jesus was taken to the holiest of cities, Jerusalem, and placed on the holiest of places, the Temple, and quoted to from the holiest of books, the Scripture. If God was present anywhere, God should be there. If Jesus was the Son of God, the fulfillment of the promise of Israel, all of sacred tradition would say that where God is most present no harm should come to one who is faithful to God.

The cleverness of the temptation was that the Devil did quote Scripture accurately (Psalms 91:11-12), which suggests that the most sacred of tradition can be used to distort one's ministry even in the most sacred of places. One cannot hide behind scriptural quotes or sacred places. Jesus' response was to quote Deuteronomy 6:16, "Do not put the Lord your God to the test, as you tested him at Massah." This makes reference to Exodus 17:1-7 where the people of Israel became desperate for water in the wilderness and began to rebel against Moses and, by implication, God. Moses, following God's guidance, struck a rock and water came forth. They called the place Massah, because they put the Lord to the proof by saying, "Is the Lord among us or not?" (Exodus 17:7). Jesus was recognizing that the need to call upon God for signs of God's faithfulness is itself an indication of one's lack of faith in God. Later, in the Garden of Gethsemane, Jesus demonstrated awareness that he had access to such Divine power (26:53), but the very act of calling upon it would distort the fulfillment of the purpose of God.

The question before the Body of Christ, is: "Are we God's servant, or do we seek to make God our servant?" Do we look at events in terms of how they serve or threaten our perceived needs or how they can fulfill God's purpose?

The third temptation of ministry is to make our service to others as the means by which we gain status and authority over other people. It is a way of serving others while still being in charge.

When Jesus came "up" out of the water, having identified with the struggle of the people, he was led "up" by the Spirit into the wilderness and then he was taken "up" to a very high mountain and shown all the kingdoms of the world and the glory of them. If he was tempted to prove himself better than Moses and Elijah by being the source of bread for the hungry, and if he was tempted to display his access to God's power in a spectacular display, now he was tempted to assume the real reigns of power. If one is going to identify with the struggle of people, as Jesus did at baptism, then is it not natural to want to assume the reigns of power whereby you can really effect change in their lives? By this temptation, Satan exposed himself as well. Satan, the adversary of God, is the desire to display power over people. Jesus was demonstrating that God was revealed not in lording it over people but by serving them in ways that give them freedom. Jesus' response to the temptation to assume power over people was to quote Deuteronomy 6:13 which committed him to giving worth or worship only to God. Thus he identified the temptation of power to be a form of idolatry.

The continual temptation for people who are used to having power in their lives is to want to gain identity by "doing" something-- feeding, jumping, controlling--rather than by "being" what God calls one to be.

Each of the three temptations was a distortion of potentially legitimate pursuits on behalf of others. Later Jesus would feed the hungry, display access to God's power, and exercise authority over others, but these acts came out of his identity centered in God and not in pursuit of that identity.

Silencing the Call to Repentence

Matthew was not naive in believing that those who have power will welcome such a gospel easily. In fact such a gospel will be seen as a threat to many who now experience benefits from the present world's arrangements Matthew was proclaimed a gospel in which the world's view of power relationships was turned upside down. It required repentance, or a complete reversal of orientation, if one was to experience the true presence of God operating in this world. John the Baptist proclaimed the necessity of such repentance if one was going to be prepared to receive the kingdom of heaven that was even then entering the world. In 4:12-17, John was arrested and no word of protest was heard from Jerusalem's leaders. The politics of power, as seen in Herod and the religious leaders, began to silence John's call to repentance. For both the secular and the religious powers, such a call to repentance was a challenge to their current accommodation with the world as it existed.

What happens when people who are in power refuse to respond to the call to change their way of life?

Matthew described Jesus, the living presence of God, responding to the arrest of John by withdrawing to the hills of Galilee--Galilee of the Gentiles (4:12 ff). Normally this fringe province of Judea, with its heavily pagan element living there, would not have been considered as the center of God's revelation. Anything revealing God would have been expected to come from Jerusalem and the Temple. Jesus established residence in Capernaum by the sea which, according to 9:1, became "his own town." The Messiah did not dwell in Jerusalem but in Capernaum. Matthew saw this as a fulfillment of the prophecy of Isaiah 9:1-2. Isaiah was recalling the time recorded in 2 Kings 15:29 when because of the disobedience of the king, Pekah, the land of Zebulum and Naphtali had been captured by Assyria and foreign people were settled on the land, thus giving it the name of Galilee of the Gentiles. If the people refused to be obedient to God, Isaiah declared, God's Word could move to the fringe of the territory, to Galilee of the Gentiles, and there light would shine. Matthew saw the same thing happening in Jesus' moving to Galilee in response to the disobedience of those in Jerusalem.

It is natural to protect one's position in the world, but in doing so one may miss what God is doing.

Since the centers of religion and secular power would not allow the necessary preparation for the revelation of God's presence, it was revealed at the edge. The revelation of God's Word would not be denied. At the same time there

IT IS NATURAL TO PROTECT ONE'S POSITION IN THE WORLD, BUT IN DOING SO, ONE MAY MISS WHAT GOD IS DOING.

was a strong warning to those who exercise power in this world that their response would determine whether they would be aware of what God was doing. In describing this incident, Matthew was preparing his hearers for the reason why they (we) must be sensitive to the powerless in this world if they wished to know what God was revealing.

From Matthew's perspective, people, then and now, became so conditioned by their culture that they arrest the call to repentance and shut God out of the very center of their existence and activity. When that happens for an individual or for a people, God withdraws to the fringe of life, the pagan elements in life, the pieces that do not fit life as we imagine it. It is the foreign element, that which disrupts life as we think it should be, which creates a crack in the impregnable fortress we have created and allows new light to shine through. The urban merchants and landowners of Matthew's day, and any of us who are continually tempted to consolidate our positions in faith and life, are thus warned of the necessity of repentance which could enable anyone to be open to God's word. We are also alerted to the necessity of being open to that which we might be tempted to dismiss as pagan or impure as the religious leaders in Jesus' day dismissed that which was happening in Galilee.

The Kingdom-Like Response

Can one live in this world without using what power one has to protect oneself?

In 5:5 Jesus spoke of the meek inheriting the earth. It was Jesus who had to flee to Egypt, not Herod. Later it would be Jesus who hung upon the cross, not Caesar. The world seemed always to give way to the strong. Psalms 37:10-11 says, "Yet a little while, and the wicked will be no more;... But the meek shall inherit the land, and delight themselves in abundant prosperity." Jesus suggested that for those who wished to share in the ministry of God's kingdom, the psalmist was more accurate than those who sought to shape the world by force. Yet, by Jesus' own experience, it was clear that there was a cost to such a commitment.

Why should Christians choose to turn the other cheek?

The intention behind such kingdom-like responses, even in the face of conflict, is made clear in 5:38-42. The law, "an eye for an eye and a tooth for a tooth," had been a step forward in civilizing the destructive response to personal conflict. It had the effect of limiting retribution or not allowing vengeance to go beyond an equal response to the offense committed. But Jesus saw God's will as going beyond retaliation and seeking reconciliation. "Do not resist an evildoer." To resist evil when it is committed against the self is to generate violence and spread the evil further. Only when you have the strength and the freedom to choose to absorb the violence done against you is there any possibility that the violator will pause to reflect that there is something different here. While many people are quick to recommend such a lesson to the abused of the world when in frustration they rebel in violence against the structures of society which have repressed them, Matthew was saying that it was precisely those who were in a position of power who needed to make the kingdom-like response to those who had responded to them in violence. It was upon those who had access to power, as did Jesus, that a healing response was asked. That healing response begins by voluntarily refusing to use the power at one's command to protect the self at the expense of the violator. It is only then that the violator is confronted by the reality that there is something different here than the same old power game.

Jesus gave four examples in ascending order of conflict. First he provided a response to personal conflict: "If anyone strikes you on the right cheek..." To be struck on the right cheek would be especially vicious, because it would mean the violator struck you with the back of the hand rather than the palm. For a person who has the power to do otherwise to make an unexpected response of offering the other cheek instead of retaliation is to offer the offender the opportunity to recognize the presence of a new reality.

Second, Jesus posed a legal conflict in which the violator would sue you for your coat. Within the legal system within the Middle East at the time of Jesus, it was an accepted reality that a judge would accept a gift in return for a favorable decision. Therefore, the judicial system favored the rich and the powerful. The law of Israel took a stand against such procedures but was not entirely successful. Prophets, like Amos, railed against such practices in Israel: "...you who afflict the righteous, who take a bribe, and push aside the needy in the gate(Amos 5:12b)." But as with the law restricting retaliation, the most that the plaintiff could hope for was equal justice. If the person who sued you saw you respond by offering your cloak as well, she would experience a reality that went beyond all legal expectations even within Israel (Exodus 22:26).

Third, Jesus described an institutional conflict. By the laws of occupation, a Roman soldier could conscript a citizen to carry his pack for a certain distance. This would have been particularly humiliating for a person who possessed wealth or power. For such a person to go voluntarily an extra distance would be not grudging compliance but a genuine act of kindness that could witness both to the soldier and the fellow citizen that something new was present here.

Fourth, he raised the economic conflict which often separated citizen from citizen. The beggar who fit into the lowest class of an agrarian society and the borrower who had fallen on hard times were both to be responded to with an openness which contradicted the normal possessiveness of society. Those who had been blessed in this world were to "give to everyone who begs from you, and do not refuse anyone who wants to borrow from you."

As Jesus' entire life would indicate, participation within the reign of God means neither avoiding people who might violate you nor responding to them in kind. Instead of using one's power to serve oneself, participation in the kingdom provided one the base of freedom out of which one could choose to act in an unexpected way that would cause a violator to sense the presence of something new. Jesus' vision was not that of just passively absorbing but of choosing to act in ways that offered the violator a future. Like all acts of God's rule, this would not force a certain response but invited the person to enter into a new realm which could restore humanness.

> WHY WOULD GOD ASK PEOPLE TO LIVE IN A WAY THAT WOULD LIKELY RESULT IN SUFFERING?

Why would God ask people to live in a way that would likely result in suffering?

The purpose of restoring the lost sheep of Israel was to prepare them for a mission to the world which could not be accomplished through the exercise of power. They were to be sent as sheep on a mission to a world of ravenous wolves. In 10:16-23 Matthew made clear that Jesus knew that both the religious authorities ("...they will hand you over to councils and flog you in their synagogues") and the secular authorities ("...and you will be dragged before governors and kings because of me...") would be threatened by those who followed him. But Jesus also knew that such situations would also be unique opportunities to bear "testimony to them and the Gentiles" of an alternate reality. If his followers were wise as serpents, wise enough to look for opportunities in the midst of the evil done to them, and innocent as doves, innocent enough not to let the bitterness of their suffering blind them, then God's spirit could speak through them even to people in power: "For what you are to say will be given to you at that time." Matthew was not asking his congregation to passively suffer but to be prepared to creatively suffer in a way that confronted those in power with an alternate reality.

An Alternate Reality

There are those today who either look for a divine intervention that will correct all wrong in the world or for a combination of religious and political leadership that will assume the reigns of power and defeat those who oppose the faithful.

In contrast to the use of naked power to force obedience, Jesus offered an alternate vision of how God operates in the universe as expressed in his prayer of thanksgiving in 11:25-30. "I thank you,... because you have hidden these things from the wise and the intellegent and have revealed them to infants;..." In a world in which wisdom was often made the servant of the powerful, Jesus gave thanks that God had chosen to disrupt the patterns of the powerful through acts of grace. Grace is that experience of receiving special blessings without respect to one's abilities or insights. Such grace democratizes the universe and lifts up the weak and the helpless. For Matthew Jesus embodied that grace in his ministry and thus identified with God as Father and received God's identification with him as Son. It is not understanding wisdom but understanding grace that is the key to unlocking the universe:"All things have been handed over to me..." Therefore "all you that are weary and are carrying heavy burdens" can find rest in Jesus who is the source of grace that releases one to wholeness. It is true that Christians are called to resist and transform the evil powers and structures that oppress and distort both people and the universe. But no matter what structures they change or reforms they institute, both Christians and non-Christians will move from slavery to slavery until they discover the power of grace that lifts them up and makes them whole even before the universe is transformed.

We are invited to participate in an alternate reality.

That alternate reality to which the followers of Jesus were invited could be introduced into the world only in a condition of freedom. God refused to impose the kingdom on the world by force. If one accepted the standard translation of 10:34-36, "I have not come to bring peace, but a sword," then it would appear that Jesus was continuing to prepare his disciples for a negative response to the gospel brought about by the fact that it forced people to make difficult choices. Jesus was saying there could be a false peace based purely on the absence of conflict because of the absence of choices, but this then resulted in oppression. This fake peace was in contrast to Jesus' message that, like a sword, cuts the bonds of oppression but thereby can encounter conflict from those who had vested interest in the present state of bondage.

W. F. Albright and C. S. Mann in their *Anchor Bible Commentary on Matthew* offer a strong case, however, for an alternate translation whose meaning would be consistent with the rest of Jesus' message as recorded in Matthew: "Do not think that I have come to impose peace on earth by force; I have come neither to impose peace, nor yet make war." If this translation is accurate, Jesus was dismissing two popular expectations of messiahship. Some expected a messiah who would utilize divine power to impose God's will on the world; while others looked for a messiah who would be a military leader that would lead God's nation in conquest of other nations.

Matthew saw Jesus as refusing to force God's rule on either Jews or Gentiles. Instead Jesus recognized that the truth he proclaimed would result in painful choices even within families. If this translation is correct, it would be consistent with Jesus' rejection of the temptation to power (4:8-10). Further it would be a recognition of the truth of John's proclamation that the Messiah's presence would result in a winnowing process (3:11-12).

The Fruit of Power

At the same time it is clear that we cannot operate in this world without exercising power. The critical issue is what are the fruits of our use of power.

Though Matthew's congregation is to resist the temptation to see power as good in itself or to use it as a means of

BY THEIR FRUITS, YOU SHALL KNOW THEM.

protecting Christians at the expense of others, they will exercise power in this world. The question is how should one exercise power in life? When Jesus acted in power, in the healing of the blind, dumb demoniac in 12:22-30 for example, the question was raised as to the source of his power. The Pharisees immediately suggested that he acted by the power of the chief of demons. We who experience so many cults which promise the miraculous should be sympathetic to the Pharisees' concern. The question was not whether Jesus acted with a power from beyond the human dimension but whether the source of that power was good or evil. Jesus' familiar response was "...the tree is known by its fruit." Even evil has to be true to itself. If it is not, it will only weaken its own power. "No city or house divided against itself will stand." If real good is being done, then the power of evil (Satan) is being weakened.

The Pharisees were asking whether someone could, by doing good, deceive and seduce someone into evil. Jesus' response was that it was only when you began to bind a person that you had the opportunity to plunder their lives (12:29). When Jesus healed, he did not use his healing gift to bind people to himself but rather to set them free of that which bound them.

The danger of any religious movement is when it begins to bind and dehumanize rather than set people free to be more truly themselves.

Jesus thus transformed the question of the source of power into the question of its effect on people. Again it is by your fruits that you will know. The question that should be asked in exercising power is whether people are being bound or set free by the actions performed. In light of the previous controversy over the Sabbath (12:1-14) in which Jesus suggested the misuse of the Sabbath was in fact binding people, Jesus has now reversed the issue and raised questions as to the result of the power exercised by the Pharisees. Since the Pharisees were part of the religious community and not pagan outsiders, the question was raised for all those who are part of the church as to whether their ministry, no matter how sincerely performed or how accurately backed up by Scripture and tradition (recall the second temptation) results in people being released or bound.

Ministry in the Midst of Chaos

The powers against which the church must contend are not just those of rational discourse created by those who hold sincere but differing opinions.

The story in 14:1-12 of the beheading of John the Baptist illustrates what Paul talks about when he says that we are not contending with flesh and blood but rather against the principalities and power of this world. (Ephesians 6:12). When Paul refers to "principalities and powers," he is referring to the non-human forces and powers that operate on our lives and the life of our communities. On a personal basis, it would be forces like ego, lust, greed, fear, etc. On a community wide basis, it could be panic, national pride, national security, corporate survival, etc. To use a contemporary example, a corporation might choose to sacrifice the quality of their product or alter their financial reports in order to increase the quarterly profits and better position themselves in the stock market.

On a more global scale, a government might ignore the dangers of global warming because they are fearful of the response of the general public if they were to take the necessary actions to counter such a problem.

John had challenged the ethics of Herod's marriage (14:3-4, probably based on the law in Leviticus 18:16 and 20:21). Herod tried to silence this ethical challenge to his behavior by exercising his secular power to arrest (4:12). In Herod we see the common temptation of governments to use their power to silence an ethical challenge to their behavior. Yet the response of the people to John obviously put constraints on what Herod felt free to do. "Though Herod wanted to put him to death, he feared the crowd, because they regarded (John) as a prophet." Then Herodias' daughter secured a public promise from Herod to do as she wished, and she asked him to behead John. The fear of loss of face was greater than public pressure or political wisdom, and so he had John beheaded.

Herod was a Jew. It was a violation of Jewish law to execute by beheading but this practice was in line with Roman and Greek custom. Herod thus declared where his true loyalties were. When John, a popular prophet, challenged Herod's ethics, fear and the insecurity of his position caused Herod to act in a way that violated his Jewish heritage. He arrested and tried to silence a prophet. Yet John's message was popular enough among the people to constrain the unbridled use of power. Then the threat to Herod's ego of the possible loss of face in breaking a publicly made promise was strong enough to overcome even that restraint. Herod was willing not only to risk the displeasure of his people by killing John but to actually offend them by doing it in a manner forbidden to a Jew, which Herod claimed to be.

The powers at work in that incident were not just those of humans, which can be appealed to with rational arguments. Rather it was humans that were experiencing the force of the principalities of governments and the powers of ego, fear, et cetera. When ethical issues are raised with respect to the behavior of individuals or institutions, the cause of that behavior is rarely logic alone. Human behavior results from a variety of principalities and powers that vie for a position of dominance in a person's decision making.

To be the church does not mean that Christ surrounds you with a magic spell that protects you from all the contrary elements in life. In one sense, like those first disciples, the church is sent out alone to battle the forces that seek to overwhelm it.

Ministry in a world of contending powers and forces, since it is beyond the rational, is experienced as chaos. Yet Matthew saw Jesus as sending his disciples to minister in the midst of such chaos. In 14:22-27 Matthew painted a living parable of the church's relationship between faith and chaos. The disciples have been sent by boat to the other side of the lake. The boat, from the time of Noah, had been a symbol of the faithful community, and among Christians it quickly became a symbol of the church. Therefore Matthew symbolized the church and her disciples being sent out on the sea of the world.

The sea and the waters were continual symbols of chaos, which only God could overcome (Genesis 1:2 and Psalms 107:23-32). The disciples' journey was not easy, and they found themselves beaten by the waves because the winds (the conditions) were against them.

At the same time, Christ is not unmindful of his people. The promise to the church is not that the church will not be threatened by the powerful forces that surround it and make the Body of Christ look frail in comparison, like a small boat on a stormy sea, but that no matter how bad the chaos looks, God is neither overwhelmed nor unmindful of the people of faith.

At their most desperate moment, Christ came to the disciples in what appeared to be an almost supernatural way. It was so unexpected that the disciples' response was one of fear

> IN THE BEGINNING WHEN GOD CREATED ... THE EARTH WAS A FORMLESS VOID AND DARKNESS COVERED THE FACE OF THE DEEP

rather than relief. Those first disciples wondered what unearthly event was happening. Until, that is, Christ addressed us them: "Take heart, it is I, do not be afraid." Literally, "be of good cheer, I am, do not fear." In Scripture, "I am" signals a self-revelation of God (Exodus 3:14 and John 6:35). In the midst of our struggle against that which would overwhelm us, the chaotic forces of evil, we are addressed by God who is not overwhelmed, and we are claimed by Christ, the Word of God that brings order out of chaos (Genesis 1:1ff). The one who created all life addresses us through the Christ and rescues us from the fears and elements which threaten to engulf us.

All of us would like to know how to conquer the chaos that threatens to engulf us.

In 14:28-33 Matthew added the story of Peter walking on water. Peter saw Jesus coming to him on the water. Typical of Peter, he impulsively asked Jesus to ask him to come to Jesus on the water. Peter, seeing Jesus exercise lordship over the watery chaos (Genesis 1:2), wanted to share in that lordship or mastery over chaos. So, like Peter, the rock upon which the church is built (16:18), the church, occasionally, impulsively asks Christ to invite her to make a risky decision on faith in the hopes of gaining mastery over the chaos that disturbs our world. Christ said come, and Peter (the church) stepped out onto the water and began to walk toward Jesus. There was almost a giddy sensation of having taken a bold step of faith and seeing it be effective.

But even the boldest acts of faith are surrounded by the winds of doubt that seek to penetrate into the believer. Peter saw the wind, was afraid, and began to sink. Peter, the leader among the disciples, stands as a living witness that disciples can take no pride in the strength of their faith to save them. Though strong faith can enable disciples (us) to take bold steps, it is Christ, a power outside of our control, not faith, which saves disciples in times of weakness.

Thus, though we do not master the chaotic powers of the universe, we can set out to minister in the midst of them.Though each of us is called to act in faith, it is often the very human quality of doubt and fear through which God works.

We do not know what the results would have been if Peter had walked without fear or doubt toward Jesus. Then, perhaps, the witness of the church would have been to the arrogant superiority of faith. We would control the secret and possess the power to master the chaos of the universe. As it was, though faith is extremely important, it was Christ, whom we do not control, who reached out to Peter in his weakness when he cried out, "Lord, save me!" It is the power of Christ, not our faith, which saves us. Peter was again restored to the boat, or the community of faith, and the troubling winds ceased. It is that very strength from beyond that comes to disciples like Peter in times of doubt that is the real witness to others. "And those in the boat worshiped him, saying, 'Truly you are the Son of God.'" By faith we walk on water. In doubt, we discover Christ's witnesses through us to God's sustaining love. Again Matthew made clear that God's revelation was experienced at the point where people were weak in faith as well as where they were strong.

The Tranfiguration of the Politics of Faith

God is not defeated by our imperfections. Rather God chooses to be made known in a church filled with strengths and weaknesses.

The full implication of this inversion of power politics was only revealed to the disciples after Peter had confessed Jesus as the Christ (16:16). In 17:1-8, Peter, James, and John were led up a high mountain. These disciples were not drawn from the powerful and the wise but from the marginal fishermen of Galilee. James and John were temperamental and power hungry (20:20ff). Peter, by his impulsive and erratic behavior, suggested that the church was advanced by the gift of faith (16:17), not the insight of clever leadership. This representative body of humanity, with its gifts and weaknesses, was invited by Jesus to draw apart to encounter God.

For Matthew's congregation, many of whom gained status in the world through their striving and cleverness, it was a lesson in humility. Jesus was the equalizer who leveled the hierarchy of faith that suggested only the elite could meet God. Like certain prominent religious figures of our day, the high priest was imputed a purity that exemplified godliness. But now it was not a high priest, who once a year trembled as he drew close to God by entering the holy of holies in the Temple, but common folk, who often stumble even as they follow Jesus.

Jesus was transfigured before them, and "his face shown like the sun, and his clothes became dazzling white." The face shining echoes the description of Moses' talking with God on a mountain (Exodus 34:29-35). As with Moses, it was a reflection of the divine intimacy of conversing with God as a friend (Exodus 33:11). The garments being "dazzling white" recalls Malachi 3:2, which speaks of the coming of God to God's Temple. Only now, consistent with Matthew's understanding of the effect of Christ's ministry, the real temple where God dwells is the world, as seen by the mountain. The priests are now not part of a hierarchy but from the common folk with their combinations of faith and misunderstanding.

The context of the words of Malachi was that of the prophet lashing out at the wealthy who went through the rituals of faith but oppressed the weak from their positions of power. Then Malachi told them of the coming of God in judgment and reminded them of the laws of Moses that stood against such oppression. He also proclaimed that, prior to God's coming, Elijah, the prophet, would come to reconcile some of the divisions of the world. Now these fishermen saw Moses and Elijah, the Law and the Prophets, talking with Jesus who had fulfilled the Law and the Prophets by siding with the needy and the common folk.

The politics of the religious world are turned upside down when the unlearned and the sinful, as represented by these disciples, discovered the meaning of the Law and the Prophets ahead of the scribes and the priests. It would be the fishermen who would teach the scholars and not vice versa. Priests and ministers would look to their congregations, or even to those outside the congregation, in order to learn the purpose of God. The transfiguration of Jesus was the transfiguration of the politics of faith. The concept of hospitality in the Middle East is essential to understanding Peter's response to this vision of Moses and Elijah talking to Jesus. Rabbinic tradition said Moses did not die, and Scripture says Elijah was taken up into heaven via a flaming chariot. Now these two representatives of the best of Israel's faith, symbolic of the Law and the Prophets, are seen conversing with Jesus. By offering to erect tents for them, Peter was demonstrating hospitality for these three distinguished figures. To show hospitality is to put aside one's own interests and make room for the needs and desires of your guest. Peter was not seeking something for himself but was seeking to serve his guests by creating shelter for them.

The church that wishes to experience the presence of the living Christ in its midst must offer hospitality to the needy.

When Abraham showed hospitality to three strangers by the oaks of Mamre, he encountered God (Genesis 18:1ff). So now as Peter demonstrated hospitality, he too encountered God. The bright cloud that overshadowed them was a reference to the bright cloud of Exodus 40:34-38, which marked the presence of God in the newly constructed tabernacle. Only now Jesus is the tabernacle where God resides. Echoing Psalms 2:7, as well as the voice from heaven that confirmed Jesus at baptism (3:17), now a voice from the cloud of God's presence confirmed Jesus to be the true revelation of the divine as a faithful son reflects the father. Though attested to by the Law and the Prophets, it was Jesus of whom God said, "Listen to him!" The divine authority was not to be constrained by traditional interpretations of the Law and the Prophets but was to be re-presented in all its radicalness by a living presence.

The response of the church to those rare mountaintop experiences is often one of fear and awe.

The disciples' response to the realization of what was in their midst was a response of fear and awe. "But Jesus came and touched them saying, 'Get up and do not be afraid.'" In Christ they were made bold to act in response to the divine mystery. They were not able to comprehend all that God was, but in Jesus they were given a pure and undistorted reflection that enabled them to choose, without fear, to live life according to God's purpose. "And when they looked up, they saw no one except Jesus alone." The Law and the Prophets had been summed up in Jesus. There was no excuse of fear and blindness--their eyes had been opened. When the church is touched by the Divine, it hears Christ say, "Now rise--stand in your God-given dignity."

The Experience of Powerlessness

How does the church use its authority?

Following the vision, it was necessary for the disciples to appropriate the significance of the vision into real life by coming back down the mountain (17:9). As they came down the mountain, Jesus commanded them, "tell no one about the vision until after the Son of Man has been raised from the dead." This warning is usually explained as Jesus' desire to keep the messiahship secret until he reached Jerusalem. Yet, to the church, the warning must also speak to the use of authority.

How often is a religious community tempted to use a spiritual vision or religious experience to command conformity to their understanding of truth?

A spiritual vision may, as it did for these three disciples, confirm the truth of the direction of one's journey of faith. But such a vision must not become the authority by which one conveys the faith to others. When the church uses the gift of spiritual visions in that manner, it becomes a source of power by which she lords it over others in the manner of the Gentiles (20:25). The raising of the Son of Man from the dead, on the other hand, will not be a private experience, but one that can be appropriated even by the powerless and therefore is not the exclusive possession of the powerful.

The hope of the church is to become true disciples by participating in this transformation of the politics of faith.

When Jesus was asked who was the greatest in the kingdom of heaven, he chose a child as a reflection of greatness (18:1-4). If he was intending to speak against the hierarchy of power to which the world seduces us, then the child was an effective image. A child was the most vulnerable, and by many considered to be the most useless, member of Jesus' society. It was not the child's innocence, innate goodness, or trust, but the child's vulnerability that caused it to be such an effective image.

"Unless you change and become like children..." the phrase signifies repentance--a total about face. Instead of trying to increase your control over the world, as is natural as one passes

WHAT DO CHILDREN HAVE TO TEACH US ABOUT ENTERING THE KINGDOM OF GOD?

from childhood to adulthood, one must do an about face and be willing to become vulnerable to the pain that even the weakest and least powerful feel in this world (20:25-27) if one is to reflect God's Kingdom. This is because that is exactly the way God acts. God refuses to overpower the wicked but instead chooses to identify with the victims in their pain and suffering.

Why must one experience powerlessness in life in order to understand how God operates in this world?

There is a humility known only to those who are subject to the whims of the powerful that enables people of faith to recognize the place of trust in their relationship with God. There is no question that the world provides us with contradictory experiences of suffering and injustice. What Jesus declared in such a world was that our only hope was to become like a child. Children place trust in parents not because the parents always appear to be just or understanding, but because the parents are their only true hope. They see hope in the relationship that overcomes the questions that might be raised by the contradictory experience. Greatness in the kingdom of heaven, or God's reformed future, was making itself felt in Jesus. It could only be experienced by those who trusted in that relationship, despite all appearances which might tempt them to the contrary. Intuitively, they knew that the builder of that society was the only true hope. For the church, such a story becomes a choice of whom they (we) really trust in bringing about the desired future.

Reversal of Vengence

How vulnerable can we expect the church community to become when someone deliberately offends or takes advantage of it?

In one sense the rabbinic law put the burden of action on the offender. The offender must repent, apologize, and make reparation and only then must the injured party forgive. But Jesus put the burden of action on the injured party when he told Peter that he must forgive seventy times seven in 18:21-22. Whereas in Genesis 4:24 the vengeance laid claim to by humans seemed to be limitless ("If Cain is avenged sevenfold, truly Lamech seventy-seven fold."), now the forgiveness expected of the Christian community for one another was to be limitless (seventy times seven). Just as Pentecost is seen as the beginning of the reversal of the Tower of Babel, so here Matthew recorded the reversal of vengeance. Jesus established a community that by the intimacy of their relationships, the length they were willing to go toward healing the rupture of conflict (18:15-17), and their unlimited willingness to forgive reversed the conditions expressed in the claim of the right of vengeance by Lamech

(Genesis 4:24). It begins within the community and spreads out into the world.

It is natural to believe that if you are too forgiving, you will be taken advantage of.

Peter's question "Lord, if another member of the church sins against me, how often should I forgive?" laid bare the skepticism of being taken advantage of by others. What if one forgave and one's companion in the faith refused to take serious responsibility for the offensive act and just continued to offend? Was not the old Jewish law better whereby the offender had to first demonstrate having taken responsibility for the full seriousness of the act through repentance, apology and restitution, and then one forgave? Otherwise one's forgiveness would not really mean anything, would it? Jesus' response provided an image of the mission of the church. Jesus' insistence on unlimited forgiveness was not based on the human desire to call someone who had offended us to account. Rather, it was based on the mandate of the Christian community to reflect the character of God who offers unlimited forgiveness.

New Concept of Dominion

The temptation for the church is always to want to cooperate with the powers of society in order to receive favorable treatment and avoid suffering.

Certainly that was the temptation facing Matthew's urban merchants and middle class people whose security in society depended upon the favorable reception of the powerful elite.

Jesus made three predictions of his coming death and resurrection. The physical movement of these predictions was from the northern most city of Jesus' travels through Galilee (of the Gentiles) to Jerusalem, the focus of religious power in Israel. In the first prediction made in Caesarea Philippi (16:21), Jesus suggested that it was "he" who must go to Jerusalem and suffer at the hands of the Sanhedrin, but by the second prediction (17:22-23), made in Galilee, Jesus said that it was the "Son of Man" who would be killed by men. In the third prediction, as Jesus was going up to Jerusalem (20:17-19), he selected the twelve representatives of the "New Israel" who must go with him and the "Son of Man" would be condemned to death by the "Sanhedrin" and crucified by the "Gentiles." Jesus, who for Matthew embodied the reconciliation of the Jew and the Gentile world, along with the church as represented by the twelve, first had to experience rejection by both.

In the apocalyptic thought of the time, as represented in Daniel 7:13-14, the Son of Man was the title of the one whom God chose to rule over all the kingdoms and conquer all unjust power, and through him Israel would rule over the world (Daniel 7:27). Now Jesus claimed the title, Son of Man. Jesus' moving through the Gentiles toward Jerusalem, the presumed seat of his power, suggested that both the religious elite and the Gentiles would reject him and condemn him to death, and yet he would be raised up.

Jesus shattered the normal concept of dominion as conceived by those who heard the title "Son of Man." Dominion comes not through alliance with powers of religion or politics, who usually are in a symbiotic relationship with each other, but through exercising faithfulness to God's call even in the light of likely suffering and death.

The promise of the resurrection, which Jesus reiterated after each prediction of his coming suffering and death, was not to be seen as just a hope of personal survival in the hereafter but as an affirmation by God for those who are willing to see suffering on behalf of others as a vocation. Isaiah 53:1-12, often referred to as the fourth servant song, promised that a person or community who voluntarily accepted the suffering even unto death would be raised by God in affirmation of such faithfulness. Jesus lived in response to that promise and both experienced and revealed to others God's confirmation of his faithfulness. Now Matthew's congregation, and many Christian congregations around the world who today face the reality of suffering in response to their faith, is invited to witness to God's faithfulness in the same manner. The disciples (the church) were called to look beyond the feelings of distress when faced with threat and suffering and to open themselves to the resurrection possibility. This was not so that they could triumph over their opposition but precisely so that they could live on behalf of those who oppose and feel judged by them.

This concept of dominion through faithfulness, especially in the light of likely suffering and death, is particularly difficult for any of us who presently experience some control in our lives and desire to avoid suffering in life.

It was not unusual among the ruling class for a mother to intervene on behalf of a son to secure a position of power. In 1 Kings 1:11-21 there is an example of Bathsheba intervening on behalf of Solomon.

> CHRIST OFFERS A UNIQUE CONCEPT OF DOMINION; TO RULE THROUGH SERVICE.

In 4:21-22 there is evidence that James and John were from a family with sufficient resources to own their own boat and hire helpers. The temptation of the merchant class was to emulate the ruling class. Now in 20:20-23, consistent with the palace intrigue that often happened within the ruling class, it was the mother of James and John who approached Jesus to try to secure for them positions of power in the new kingdom. Like any of us, they were interested in securing their future.

In recording Jesus' response, Matthew described Jesus asking them if they were able to drink the cup that he was to drink. In Scripture the cup was not only a symbol of dominion (Psalms 23:5) but also a symbol of God's judgment (Isaiah 51:17-22 and Psalms 75:8), and suffering (Habakkuk 2:15). The disciples, who thought they were accepting a cup of royalty, were in fact going to accept the same experience of suffering that Jesus was about to enter. The dominion that is referred to is the dominion of God, which is often received not through palace intrigue but through being willing to accept the vocation of suffering on behalf of others.

The dominion that belongs to humanity is a dominion of stewardship that begins in Genesis (Genesis 1:26-31) and is a consistent theme throughout the Bible.

The way in which one exercises that dominion with respect to human relationships, as Jesus will shortly describe, is one of servanthood. That is, true dominion is not authority over other humans but responding to their needs in ways that release their potential in the same way that one cultivates the ground in order to release the plants' potential (Genesis 2:15).

For the congregation of faith, the issue of gathering power and its use in relation to others, or its diffusion for the sake of others, has always been difficult.

God does seem to assign positions of power to some in this world, and the question is whether they exercise it with a dominion which reflects the stewardship of their position or with a dominion that turns the cup into a cup of wrath, (Isaiah 51:17). The final irony will be that those who are actually at Jesus right and left when he comes into his kingdom are two robbers (20:23 and 27:44).

Servants of One Another

The vision is of a whole community in which everyone refused to think of themselves first but rather focused on being servant to the needs of others.

When in 20:24-28 the other ten disciples heard about James' and John's "grab for power," they immediately illustrated the effect of such power struggles by becoming indignant at the two brothers. To grasp the full impact of what Jesus said in response to this incident, you need to remember the structure of the agrarian society in which these people lived. Society was clearly stratified into classes, and the "rulers of the Gentiles," or the ruling elite, were so separated from the peasant and lower urban classes that there was almost no communication between them. To the ruling elite, the lower classes were subhuman and good only for creating the produce which was taxed to the benefit of the upper class. Taxes, as much as 50% to 66%, were levied in order that the ruling elite might consume the produce or use it to trade for luxury items. If Matthew was writing to an upper urban class congregation, they would have been very familiar with and probably shared in the benefits of such a society.

In such a society, where there was almost no mobility between classes, for Jesus to suggest that "...whoever wishes to be first among you must be your slave;" would be to challenge the very structure of society. A servant or slave was considered by the agrarian world to have only one function, and that was to serve the needs of the upper class who "owned" them.

This was the type of dominion of which Jesus spoke as he referred to himself as the Son of Man. In doing so, he broke open the apocalyptic image of "The Son of Man" which had taken on the connotation of royalty and replaced it with Ezekiel's usage of the term which carried the connotation of "truly human" as opposed to the majesty of God (Ezekiel 2:1 and Psalms 8:4). The Son of Man was one who was truly human and a servant of the dominion of God. The authentic human "came not to be served but to serve." And in that process, in the same way that a slave was considered to live his or her life solely for the benefit of the master's family, Jesus gave his life as a ransom for many. Jesus' life was the price to buy a world out of slavery and make all people part of the upper class, that is, fully dignified humans who were equal to all other humans. As his followers, this was and is the task of all disciples.

Risking Privilege

What is the purpose of risking yourself on behalf of others and how much risk should you take?

When Jesus said that one must renounce privilege with respect to each other and become as a slave to one another, the question would naturally arise as to how far such risk taking was to go. It was one thing to renounce class privilege while one was relating within the community of faith, but in public such behavior might risk one's very survival. In 20:29-34 Jesus, accompanied by a great crowd, was headed toward Jerusalem. The time was that of Passover when a large international crowd of Jews thronged to Jerusalem. The celebration of the Passover fanned the flame of Jewish identity and could not help but inflame resentment at the Roman colonial masters. Part of the concluding liturgy celebrating the Passover was a prayer that as God had once freed the slaves from Egypt, so, by next year at this time, may God free them from the Romans.

In this sort of tense atmosphere between the Roman occupation force and the Jews, Jesus' journey was interrupted by the shouts of two blind men beside the road shouting "Lord, have mercy on us, Son of David!" Being blind beggars who sat beside the road, they would have fallen into the class of expendables within the agrarian society. Their survival was largely dependent on the Jewish awareness of God's demand to help the weak and helpless. Such help, however, was usually rendered through alms giving and certainly not at risk to one's own well being. Now here was Jesus on a journey of immense importance being hailed with just the sort of messianic title that could get him arrested by nervous Roman guards.

The crowd, recognizing the danger, tried to silence the beggars, but they persisted. Jesus, at risk to himself and the purpose of his journey, responded as a servant to the two expendables and asked what he could do for them. Here he publicly acted out the admonition to be a slave to others even at risk to himself and the business that he was about. When they responded, "Lord, let our eyes be opened," Jesus was moved with compassion and touched their eyes, and they received both sight and insight--they followed him. Matthew thus urged his community to recognize that faithfulness was a way of life that risked privilege in response to those in need. In contrast to those who used religion as a privileged means of protecting self, Christians were and are to reveal Christ by risking self in response to the needs of others.

In a reversal of Matthew 25:31-46, where when you served one in need you served Christ, the opportunity is offered of being willing to risk self on behalf of those in need so that they are enabled to see Christ in you.

Choosing Justice

We are called to identify with the needy because, until the world addresses their need, that is where God is at work.

The answer to the question as to why Jesus believed that he and his followers should identify with the needy was answered by a much misunderstood parable in 21:33-46. Most commentaries treat this parable as a strict allegory with God as the landowner, the tenants as the religious leaders, the servants as the prophets, and the son as Jesus. Since Jesus did not see God as an absentee landowner and the parables are rarely allegories, it might be more fruitful to look at this parable as based on a familiar experience in life. Jesus often told stories based on familiar experiences in order to probe the deeper meaning of life.

> LETTING OTHERS SEE CHRIST IN YOU.

In an agrarian society, it was not uncommon for the upper class to own large tracts of land that they rented to peasants to cultivate. The landlords not only did not do the work, they did not even come in contact with the land or those who worked it but merely sent their servants to collect the rent.

The description of the vineyard in the parable is based on Isaiah 5:1-10 where Isaiah pronounces God's judgment against the injustice caused by the securing of large landholdings at the expense of others (Isaiah 5:8). Now Jesus applies the judgment of Isaiah to the large landholders of his day. Because of our tradition of property rights, we are immediately horrified by the behavior of the tenants who refuse to give the harvest to the landowner. We do not even stop to question before we judge the tenants in the wrong. What we fail to understand is that Jesus had stepped right into the midst of a basic division within his society. On the one side of the dividing line were the wealthy and the religious leaders who often served to legitimate the way of life of the wealthy. Both the wealthy and the religious leaders disdained contact with the working peasants and considered them somewhat subhuman. Both would have immediately identified with the owner as is evidenced by their response in verse 41, "...he will put those wretches to a miserable death..."

On the other side were the more vulnerable in society, with whom Jesus often identified, who would have raised a different set of questions upon hearing Jesus' description of the situation. "How did the landowner get that piece of property?" "Did he foreclose on a loan that had been given at exorbitant interest rates?" This was a very common method of securing more land. "How high was the rent on the peasants who did all the work while the landowner lounged in luxury in a far away country?"

When the servants who came to collect the rent were thrown out, some of the working class would have seen that as a beginning of a rebellion against injustice and an oppressive landlord. Such rebellions were fairly common within agrarian societies. For Matthew such activity would be consistent with the tradition of the Exodus event where God worked to liberate the oppressed. The owner's sending of his son would be seen as a tense moment in the parable. Much of the control of the agrarian system, in which the rich grew richer off the backs of the poor, was reinforced by a psychological acceptance of the system. In the sending of the son, the owner was bringing the aura of the "natural order" of the elite over the peasant to bear on the situation. The anger against the owner's servants, who were similar in class to the tenants, was one thing, but "they will respect my son." However, like the first born in Egypt (Exodus 12:29-32), the son's presence was no barrier to the ongoing revolt of the tenants.

We, who are horrified by personal violence and tolerant of a system which violates the rights of the poor, are immediately sure that no good can come out of any revolt of those who feel oppressed. It is a shock to see that we are identifying with the chief priests and elders against Jesus.

We agree with the chief priests and the elders, "the owner will put those wretches to a miserable death, and lease the vineyard to other tenants who will give him the produce at the harvest time." After all, that's what peasants are for: to produce fruits for the absentee landowners.

We are shocked to hear Jesus respond by quoting Psalms 118:22-33. "The stone which the builders rejected has become the cornerstone; this was the Lord's doing, and it is amazing in our eyes." The psalm is one of thanksgiving to God for deliverance from oppression. Jesus' response was clearly in contention with those who have just responded in support of the landowner. He was saying that those whom they rejected would be the cornerstone of God's reformed future. The fact that the chief priests and the Pharisees of verse 45, or the elders of verse 23, had failed to stand for the type of justice which would have made such violence unnecessary meant that they would be unable to participate in God's future. It was only if they identifed with the cause of justice, which was militated against by the society's values as evidenced by the parable, that they could share in the creation of God's future. Otherwise, God would take the rejected, as God had done before in Egypt, and form a new people who would produce the fruits of justice.

The Pharisees and the chief priests understood that Jesus was denouncing their alliance with the world as it was (21:4-5), but they were afraid to arrest him because the multitudes of the common folk recognized that he was speaking on their behalf. Jesus was acting as the prophets had always done by speaking out against injustice. For Matthew's hearers, as part of the merchant class which stood in the middle and had contact with both the ruling elite and the working class, the challenge was to choose with whom they would identify. Jesus' parable suggested that it was only by working to remove the inequitable structures that we could participate in God's future. To prevent violence is to remove the structures that might cause people to react with violence.

Choosing Your Authority

For most people in our churches, who are midway between the poor and the elite, the choice is a question of whether we value stability and the lack of violence more than justice for the poor and the weak.

Jesus' radical stance on behalf of the poor placed him in conflict with the Roman authorities in Matthew's society? Jesus' freedom from the various forces that operated in the world and his identification with the needy had become such a threat to those who had made accomodation with the world that strange alliances began to form. The Pharisees were offended by Jesus' freedom from the intricate religious interpretation of the Law from which they drew their power and authority. The Herodians, or members of Herod's party, who were more political in their orientation, were concerned lest the popularity of Jesus among the masses upset the careful political arrangement that they had struck with the imperial authority of Rome. Normally the Pharisees would have been more nationalistic in orientation and not pleased with the Herodian solution, but in 22:15-22 they formed an alliance. When threatened, the vested interests of religion and politics saw more to lose from the teachings of Jesus than from each other. They aligned themselves against Jesus who challenged the values of their world.

Together they approached Jesus. They began with words of praise. "Teacher, we know that you are sincere, and teach the way of God in accordance with truth and show deference to no one; for you do not regard people with partiality." Having praised Jesus, they then tried to demonstrate that such "idealistic stances" could not cope with the complexity of the real world. Having stated that Jesus speaks the truth without fear of whom he says it to, they asked him a "no-win" question: "Is it lawful to pay taxes to the emperor, or not?"

Taxes were the most vivid symbol of imperial control over the Judean province by the Romans and of the leisure classes over the working peasant. If Jesus answered "yes," then he would lose his popular stance with the nationalistic feeling of Jews who hated Roman control. He would also be giving sanction to the structure of the stratified society that allowed the elite to live off the backs of the peasants. This would be a denial of most of what Jesus had preached concerning the egalitarian relationship to be realized in God's vision of the future. But if he answered "no", he would be deliberately challenging those powers that were now in authority, and they would arrest him and thus effectively end his ministry. How can you be "wise as a serpent and innocent as a dove" in this complex world?

Jesus, aware of their intent, asked them to show him a coin, which would have been a silver denarii with the image of Caesar and the inscription which gave his name and title including the claim of divinity: "Tiberius Caesar, son of divine Augustus." When Jesus asked, they identified that the image and inscription belonged to Caesar. The image alone was considered idolatry by the Jew, and the inscription was blasphemous. By their possession of the coin, they were admitting complicity in such heresy.

When he said, "Give therefore to the emperor the things that are the emperors, and to God the things that are God's," everyone who heard could translate "Give to a false God the things that belong to a false

God." Yet no Roman could arrest him without confessing the emperor to be a false God. No wonder they marveled at this response.

We are continually having to ask whether we have attributed too much authority to the political realities that structure our lives and too little to the true God, whom we claim to be our Lord?

Responding to Violence

How would Jesus respond if people opposed him with violence and force? In 26:47-56 Judas, one of the inner circle of the faithful, came to execute his betrayal, accompanied by an armed crowd who had been sent by "the chief priests and the elders of the people." Coming up to Jesus, Judas hailed him as rabbi, again as in 26:25, avoiding the use of the term *Lord*. The kiss could be an ordinary greeting to a guest or rabbi, but Jesus refused to allow Judas to deny the intimate relationship being betrayed and said, "Friend, do what you are here to do." Judas had to take responsibility for his act.

The betrayal was not in the identification of Jesus to the crowd but in the violation of the covenant of friendship. It was the sacredness of relationships, not abstract moral values, that was revealed by the coming of the kingdom. When the bonding of friendship was violated, the deceived crowd became a mob ready to seize and destroy the presence of goodness as reflected in Jesus.

JESUS RESPONSE TO VIOLENCE

One of the disciples, still believing that courage combined with force can bring in the kingdom, drew his sword and cut off the ear of the high priest's slave. But Jesus, already having confronted the temptation to bring in the kingdom by displays of divine force (4:5-6), while recognizing that such force was available to him (Psalms 91:11-12, Matthew 13:41, and 24:31), also recognized, as he had previously taught his disciples (5:39ff), that to respond to violence with violence only perpetuated the reign of violence over human life, "All who take the sword will perish by the sword." Jesus also knew that to respond to violence with violence meant an abdication of one's freedom and allowed the other person to determine your response. This would be a diminishing of one's humanity as God would intend it within the kingdom. The kingdom brought in by force, even divine force, was a kingdom imposed on the human spirit rather than an obedient response to God made in freedom (2 Corinthians 3:17).

The power that violence has exercised over the world has been due to the fear of suffering and death.

All of the prophets and Scriptures have pointed to the fact that God's will for the world was that of relationships lived out in justice and mercy. Such a purpose had been frustrated by the human fear that had caused people to compromise justice and mercy in order to avoid their own suffering and death. For the Scriptures to be fulfilled, the grip of fear of suffering and death had to be broken. Therefore, Jesus, out of his freedom, chose to cooperate with the unfolding events and let fear and death do its worst. He recognized in the crowd's actions that the Scriptures of the prophets were being fulfilled (Zechariah 14:13) and that God's will would still not be defeated. Jesus challenged the delusion of the crowd that they were performing a mighty act by their approaching him at night with swords and clubs as if he were a dangerous criminal. He reminded them of their having listened to his teaching daily in the Temple without having found reason to seize him. He allowed fear to do its worst, because he knew it had no ability to defeat God. At the same time, he wanted to confront the crowd with their lack of freedom through their choice of violence.

The disciples, as Jesus had predicted, were scandalized by his refusal to stand and fight for what was right. For them, it may have seemed that he was simply yielding to the power of evil in this world. How could they stand with someone who refused to stand but, instead, seemed to capitulate to the power of evil before them. Not knowing how to respond, they forsook the one who appeared unwilling to fight for his own cause and fled the garden.

Truth Out of Mockery

The discovery that the center of one's truth cannot be affected by the powers of the world that seek to entrap you can release you to a new experience of freedom.

The mockery of Jesus in 27:27-31 illustrated for Matthew how, when the world most disparages truth, it often reveals it at the same time. Pilate's soldiers took the condemned criminal into the governor's residence, put a military robe on him, placed a crown of thorns upon his head, and a reed for a royal scepter in his hands. It would have been a crude burlesque, caricaturizing the image found on a Roman coin (22:20-21). Then, using the common greeting for the emperor, they cried out to him, "Hail, King of the Jews!"

In trying to make a fool out of Christ, they unknowingly spoke God's truth, again illustrating God's freedom to speak through the most unlikely of instruments. Paul would speak to the Corinthians about being "fools for Christ" (1 Corinthians 4:20) and of the foolishness of God being wiser than human wisdom and the weakness of God being stronger than human strength (1 Corinthians 1:25). Pilate's soldiers were treating Jesus as a pitiful clown. Jesus, choosing not to react to their taunts, but rather to act in freedom, became the clown of God who by his behavior, which contrasted with the way of the world, revealed the truth of God. The soldiers, unable to get the expected response, spat upon him and struck him upon the head. Still maintaining the freedom to choose how he would respond, Jesus continued to look for the will of God in the events of the moment, even those that caused him to experience ridicule.

Later, as those first Christians reflected back on the cross, they saw an image of the will of God expressed in those events. The soldier's cheap robe and

THE TRUE SOURCE OF POWER AND DIGNITY IN LIFE.

the garland of thorns became symbols of glory rather than ridicule. Behind the attempt at burlesque was revealed a deeper truth. For the urban merchants in Matthew's congregation, whose status was fragile at best and almost totally dependent on accumulating wealth, the cheap robe and thorns presented a very uncomfortable but important lesson. Merchants lived in a society that continually threatened to strip them of their dignity and mock their status, and now they were accepting a faith that questioned many of the values that they thought gave them power in life. Yet in these images, they saw the truth of God shining through all attempts at derision to such an extent that even the instruments of derision became reflectors of God's truth.

Yielding the Spirit

There will be times when one will wonder whether God has lost control, and in individual incidents even the most faithful of people will experience a dark period when they will wonder if they have been abandoned by God. Yet as Christ revealed, at such times, when we yield our spirit to God, God will not let our efforts be wasted.

At the point of the crucifixion, the question had to be asked, "Who is in charge?" Had events gotten so out of hand that God had lost control? Matthew wanted to leave no doubt, so he described that from midday until three there was darkness over all the earth. Immediately those who knew Scripture were reminded of Exodus 10:21-22 in which God commanded Moses to stretch out his hand "that there may be darkness over the land of Egypt." They would also hear the words of the prophet Amos, "And on that day," says the Lord God, "I will make the sun go down at noon, and darken the earth in broad daylight." (8:9) The forces of evil may think they are in charge of this one event, but God, who is in charge of the whole creation, the one who issues light and darkness at midday, can hardly be defeated by a single event in creation.

Jesus' final sound was a loud, inarticulate cry and a yielding up of his spirit. From the beginning (Genesis 2:7), the spirit, or breath, has been the divine source of vitality. Its source is from God (Psalms 104:30), and it is subject to God's command (Ezekiel 37:9-10). Again the emphasis is on God's being in charge, which Jesus demonstrated by yielding the last bit of control into the hands of God.

CHAPTER 2

RESPONSE TO A WORLD DIVIDED INTO FAITHFUL AND PAGAN

The universal love of God was neither an impulsive act nor a sudden change in God's plan brought about by the failure of God's people to make the desired response. Rather it was a continuing part of the work of God in history.

It is often suggested that Matthew paints Jesus as seeing his ministry as restricted to the Jewish people before the resurrection and only after the resurrection does the great universal thrust emerge in the Great Commission. Yet, when we explore the message of Matthew to his congregation, we discover that there was a consistent movement from ethnocentrism to universalism in the words and actions of Jesus as he prepared the disciples for the new creation. Jesus' message began at the level of his disciples' understanding and nurtured them toward a vision of the new creation. It was also a reminder to Matthew's people that the gospel message begins where people are but points to God's universal purpose.

The Family Tree

Matthew's Gospel begins in 1:1-17 with a family tree that lies behind the birth of the one we call the Christ. This genealogy begins with Abram (soon to be called Abraham) who was called to leave behind the normal structures of security and venture forth into a new world of God's own choosing. By the particular obedience of Abram, "all the families of the earth shall be blessed" (Genesis 12:3). Matthew indicates that, from the beginning, the revelation of God was to have worldwide significance. We know nothing about many of the people in Matthew's list, and, yet, each became a part of God's instrument of salvation. Matthew, therefore, makes clear from the beginning that the criteria by which the world evaluates the significance of someone is not the standard by which God measures either a person's worth or their value in the fulfillment of God's worldwide purpose.

Some of the names that are known, however, give us clues as to the freedom of God to work beyond the boundaries of the people of faith. In Chapter 3 we will explore the role of the feminine

> THE FREEDOM OF GOD TO WORK BEYOND THE BOUNDARIES OF THE PEOPLE OF FAITH.

in God's revelation but it is also significant that Tamar in 1:3 was not only a woman but also of non-Jewish heritage. By pointing to the torrid story of Tamar in Genesis 38, Matthew recalled for his people the extraordinary freedom by which God worked through this Canaanite woman to recall Judah, one of the patriarchs of the Jewish people, to the fulfillment of his responsibilities and thus preserved the family line through which God's anointed was born. From this Canaanite woman, who was an outcast, came one who taught us to love the outcast.

In verse five two more women of foreign origin are mentioned. The first is Rahab, the name of the prostitute who hid Joshua's spies in preparation for the Israelite invasion of the land (Joshua 2). From one who sold love for profit came one who taught us to profit from love. The second was Ruth, a Moabitess, a nation hated by Jews, who, through her loyalty to her Jewish mother-in-law, Naomi, won the love of Boaz. Because Boaz loved a member of an enemy nation, Jesse was born. It was out of the root of Jesse that the Prince of Peace was born who in turn taught us to love our enemies. These were but the first hints of the essential role of those outside the community of faith in the fulfillment of God's purpose. Though in Abraham God called a particular people to be a light unto the nations, God was also at work among people of other nations both to call Israel to faithfulness and to fulfill God's final purpose of universal salvation.

Secular Seekers of Truth

As a community of faith, should we also pay attention to those who seek truth in the secular sciences, economics, and other fields as we seek to open ourselves to God's truth?

In 2:1-12, Jesus, as the son of Abraham (1:1) by whom the whole world would be blessed (Genesis 12:3), was first recognized by wisdom seekers from the East. Two great rival powers ruled the world: Rome in the West and Parthia in the East. Mark Anthony had named Herod "King of the Jews" so that Herod might be his puppet in the buffer state between these two great powers. The Magi were people who through wisdom and observation had made themselves valuable advisors to kings. These Parthian priests, men of wealth, might risk their status with Parthia in order to gain status with Rome, but Matthew recorded them risking their lives by standing in Herod's court and announcing knowledge of a potential rival to Herod and their intention of paying homage to him.[iii] For Matthew, this was one more example of people risking status for the sake of justice and truth.

This story also illustrates the interdependence of the community of faith with those outside that community in discovering the revelation

---

[i] I am indebted to an article by Robert Coote, San Francisco Theological Seminary, for an understanding of the political significance of this event.

of God in this world. These non-Jewish seekers after truth recognized, via signs of nature, that God had broken into history in a new way. Still they had to risk everything by turning to the religious community, the keeper of the traditions, for guidance as to the actual presence of God. The religious community had failed to see the signs, and the "seekers" lacked the Scriptures to confirm the place.

When the news of Christ's birth was announced in Jerusalem, both Herod, the symbol of political power, and Jerusalem, the symbol of religious power, were troubled. Matthew thus raised the question as to whether vested interest in this world, religious or political, does not blind one to the recognition of God's activity. Almost two years after the event, neither had recognized the birth of Christ in the world. It was only in an encounter with those outside the faith that these vested interests came to recognize the possibility of this new thing that God was doing. Yet, when those completely outside the tradition made known the possibility, vested interest caused the leaders of Israel to react more with fear than joy. Unlike those in political power, here symbolized by Herod, the religious community at least knew where to look to discover the truth when they were asked the right question. But it was still the Magi, pursuing the signs that God had provided them through their pursuit of astrology, who discovered the birthplace of Jesus.

The sincerity of their search was demonstrated as they ignored all the conditions of status and fell upon their knees to worship Jesus. They offered him the wealth that formed the basis of their status. The message to Matthew's hearers, who might be tempted to protect their sometimes fragile status in society, was that by doing so they may fail to recognize the presence of God in their lives. Matthew's story about Jesus began, as it would end (27:54), with pagans recognizing the truth of Jesus while the religious community sought to do him harm. It was a haunting warning to those who would choose to be a part of the community of faith.

The Enemy as Refuge

One has to be careful about determining who our enemies are and who our friends are. Sometimes God works for our good through those whom we have named our enemies. It gives new meaning to the commandment to love our enemies.

The drama and interplay of foreigner and faithful continues in 2:13-15. The birth of Christ, the one who would represent the fulfillment of hope and goodness in this world, was perceived as an immediate threat to those in

> THE FREEDOM OF GOD TO WORK THROUGH APPARENT WEAKNESS AND EVEN AN ENEMY TO PRESERVE GOODNESS IN THE WORLD

power. If true goodness, as was seen in the Christ child, was to be sustained in this world, God had to act. So an angel of the Lord warned Joseph in a dream to take the child and his mother and flee to Egypt. Biblically, Egypt not only symbolized the oppressor but also a place of security. God communicated to an earlier Joseph through dreams (Genesis 37:5-11). The Joseph of the Genesis story was also led into Egypt in life-threatening circumstances. Only later would his family discover that when starvation threatened the very existence of the people of Israel, Egypt would be the place of their salvation (Genesis 37 and 39-45). Later, when Jesus–who for Matthew was the very fulfillment of Israel–had his life threatened, it was again by means of Joseph, this time his father, that his life was preserved in Egypt. It was incongruous for the Messiah of God to be dispossessed of his rule and forced to flee to find asylum in Egypt from his own people. Yet, it signified the freedom of God to work through apparent weakness and even a former enemy to preserve goodness in the world. God acted to save the people of the faith from themselves and did so by using pagan Egypt, symbol of oppression, as a refuge. If Matthew was speaking to Jewish Christians in pagan Antioch after both Jerusalem and the Temple were destroyed, this may well have created a glimmer of hope. God would not be defeated by such a tragedy and could work equally well among those who are unbelievers in order to accomplish the divine purpose.

Expanding the Arena of God's Activity

To participate effectively in God's kingdom, the church must participate in the ministry of reconciliation that extends beyond our comfortable religious boundaries.

In 3:1-12, John the Baptist, standing within the framework of the Hebrew prophets, proclaimed the necessity of repentance, a turning around, if one was going to be prepared to recognize God's activity in the world that was bringing about a New Creation. Part of that repentance was a repentance of narrow expectations that blinded people to God's activity. In 3:13-17, Jesus came from Galilee to the Jordan to John to be baptized by him. Contrary to narrow nationalistic expectations that the Messiah would come from Jerusalem, Jesus came from Galilee where Jew and Gentile interacted. Matthew made clear in 4:12-16 that Jesus made his home in Capernaum in fulfillment of Isaiah 9:1-2. As was mentioned in Chapter 1, the territory of Zebulun and Naphtali had been captured by Assyria who proceeded to settle refugees from other countries in that territory. The Messiah took up residence not at the center of the community of faith but in that region where Jew and Gentile, faithful and pagan, mixed. The question of religious purity, or even where one looked in order to discern the Word of God, was not as easy when one worshiped a God whose Word resided at the crossroads between the faithful and the pagan.

In 4:23 we are told that Jesus' ministry of "teaching in their synagogues and proclaiming the good news of the kingdom and curing every disease and every sickness among the people" began to bridge the gap that separated the Jewish believer from the non-believer in Jesus' world. When all three aspects of ministry were performed in the name of God, people from all over Syria (those outside the Jewish faith) and Galilee (the edge where they mixed) and Jerusalem (the center of Jewish religion) were drawn to God's Word. Those who responded to God's Word and experienced the good news in their lives expanded in both directions--back toward the center of Jesus heritage and outward towards the Gentiles in Syria (4:24-25). If there was any question among Matthew's people as to whether either the Jewish or the pagan people could be dismissed as being beyond the reach of God's care, it was now made clear that God's kingdom reconciled this difference as well.

The ministry of reconciliation includes those who have been named the enemy.

In the Sermon on the Mount, Jesus extended the concept of neighbor to include the enemy as well and thus expanded the command to "love your neighbor" so that no one could be left out (5:43-48). Christians were (are) to love their enemies in an active way–to pray that God would intercede on behalf of those very ones who actively sought to take advantage of them. The church was called to reflect God who sought to do good for those who were evil as well as good--the sun rises and rain is sent on the just and the unjust. The lines that separated the faithful and the pagan were blurred to the extent that it was impossible to know who was within and who was without.

Preparation to Receive the Word

If we do not set clear boundaries, are we not in danger of trivializing the faith?

The Jewish people had clear commandments about separating the holy from the profane. The word holy has the meaning: to be called or set apart for a divine purpose. The Hebrews were continually concerned about profaning that which was holy or set apart. Their concern was based on a belief that experiencing the holy unprepared could be dangerous. For example, they went through elaborate preparations to cleanse the people and even built a fence around Mt. Sinai when Moses talked to God (Exodus 19:9-15) to protect the people from being harmed by their encounter with the divine when they

HOLY: TO BE CALLED OR SET APART FOR A DIVINE PURPOSE

were unprepared. Today we know that people coming to Holy Scripture or a religious experience without a grounding in the community of faith can be harmed by the experience. But for some religious leaders, the danger of encountering the holy without preparation had become an excuse to separate the religious community from the larger world.

In 7:6 Jesus said: "Do not give what is holy to the dogs; and do not throw your pearls before swine, or they will trample them underfoot and turn and maul you." Dogs were considered by Jewish people to be wild beasts and pigs to be unclean, but they were also used metaphorically to refer to all heathen or pagans (15:26). By Jesus' use of this harsh sounding, perhaps familiar, proverbial saying, he appeared to be reinforcing a chauvinistic attitude whereby the Jews separated themselves from other peoples.

Understanding the danger of the misuse of religion, Jesus took this common expression of chauvinism and turned it into a command to be sensitive to the position of the unbelievers. Jesus often interacted with unbelievers and those considered to be unclean (tax collectors and sinners), but his first approach was usually an act of human kindness or concern that prepared them to receive the word of God. Without building that human relationship of genuine concern first, the word of God, which was precious like a pearl, would instead be heard either as meaningless words to be discarded and trampled underfoot or as condemnation rather than salvation. If God's word was experienced as judgment, those who heard it might turn and condemn the speaker out of defense. If the disciples (the Church) were to be the bearer of the holy word, that liberating word of God's realm of true freedom, then they should be wary of making God's word into trivial jargon.

Being "in" but not "of'" the world, the church must prepare unbelievers through acts of genuine compassion which build real relationships. Only then can they be prepared to receive that which is holy as good news for their future rather than as condemnation for their past.

This type of teaching was modeled in the second action that Matthew recorded Jesus performing following the conclusion of the Sermon on the Mount. The first had been the healing of a leper (8:1-4), which illustrated a healing and restoration of community within the community of faith. Then in 8:5-13, a Roman centurion, who represented both religious and political differences within Jesus' world, came to Jesus. For a Roman centurion to come to a Jew and ask for help was not only to recognize a reversal of roles in authority relationships but also to run a high risk of rejection by a Jew over whom he was supposed to have authority. The centurion took that risk not for himself but for a servant, which would suggest an understanding of human relationships which was far deeper than the world normally expected.

Jesus responded to the centurion's humanity by stepping outside the normal boundaries of social expectations and demonstrating "love of enemy" by offering to come to the centurion's home and healing the servant. Though not strictly against Jewish law, such behavior would have raised suspicion as to Jesus' loyalties. This demonstrated the freedom with which Jesus lived.

The centurion responded in kind with renewed humility and recognition of the power of Jesus' authority. "I am not worthy to have you come…, but only speak the word…" Drawing on his own experience in the Roman world, the centurion revealed his recognition of the power of the word spoken to effect reality. By his own response to Jesus, he elicited from Jesus an expression of the universal nature of the final or eschatological vision of God. Insight into the true nature of God's realm came not from one of those called to be a "light to the nations" but from a member of the nations.

Special Role of Restored Israel

What is the unique role of the church in the world?

In Matthew 10:5-8a, Jesus tells his disciples, "Go nowhere among the Gentiles, and enter no town of the Samaritans...," This might be seen as a contradiction to the suggested universal thrust of Matthew. Jesus, having called to him twelve disciples, named them apostles or ones sent by God on a mission. The special nature of this mission, hinted at by the number twelve, was to serve the "lost sheep of the house of Israel." Given the ease with which the early disciples entered into a mission among the Samaritans after the death of Stephen (Acts 8:2-25), this admonition cannot have been accepted by the early church as a general prohibition against mission to the Gentiles.

The clue may be in the reference to "the lost sheep of the house of Israel." In Ezekiel 34:1-16 the shepherds or religious leaders of Israel were condemned for not caring for the sheep or common people but instead profited from their condition. In an agrarian economy, the religious leaders were associated with the elite class and often served the purpose of keeping the masses content. For this service they were well paid. Ezekiel 34:4 contrasted their behavior with what God required of such religious leaders." You have not strengthened the weak, you have not healed the sick, you have not bound up the injured, you have not brought back the strayed, you have not sought the lost, but with force and harshness you have ruled them." According to Ezekiel, therefore, God would take the initiative to restore the lost sheep. So now Matthew describes Jesus initiating this action by commissioning twelve disciples as apostles of a special mission of restoration.

They were to do what the prophet Ezekiel accused the leaders of Israel of failing to do. They were to announce the nearness of the Kingdom of Heaven both in word and in deed. "As you go proclaim the good news..." and "cure the sick, raise the dead, cleanse the lepers, cast out demons" (10:7-8a). It was the Israelites, those who had wrestled with the divine dimension in their lives at times of deep distress (Genesis 32:22-32), who were prepared to recognize the presence of God in these experiences of healing. Other people might conclude that such healing was just a run of good luck, but, because of the history of their faith, the Israelites were prepared to see signs of God's presence in such experiences. In the same manner that the Magi found it necessary to go to Jerusalem, the keeper of the religious tradition, in order to understand the location of the revelation they had perceived in the stars, so the world needed Israel, the restored Israel, to help it understand what it was that they were experiencing. Jesus' special commissioning of these particular twelve to go just to the "lost sheep of the house of Israel" should not be seen as neglect or lack of concern for Gentiles or Samaritans but as a specific and special task of restoring Israel to her true vocation. Israel, when it was true to its vocation of following God, would be a blessing to the rest of the world (Genesis 12:2).

Our Response is Critical

Sometimes the actions of people outside our faith remind us of our true calling.

Jesus also used what was happening in the Gentile world to call Israel back to its true vocation. The scribes and Pharisees, who had seen Jesus exercise God's healing power to release people from that which bound them, wanted Jesus to prove himself with a spectacular display. Jesus responded that "...no sign shall be given to (them) except the sign of the prophet Jonah (12:38ff). Jonah was an Israelite prophet sent on a mission to pagan Nineveh. But just as Israel tried to escape her universal vocation, so Jonah tried to escape his vocation by sailing in the opposite direction. God went to extreme lengths, causing a storm at sea and finally having a whale swallow Jonah and return him to dry land, so that Jonah could again pursue God's

> JESUS USED WHAT WAS HAPPENING IN THE GENTILE WORLD TO CALL ISRAEL BACK TO ITS TRUE VOCATION.

calling. Building on this story, Jesus declared that God would go to extreme lengths–seemingly again violating the laws of nature as happened in the incident of the whale–in order to preserve the Son of Man, the embodiment of Israel, so as to recall Israel to obedience in its mission to the non-Israelite world.

Despite God's extreme efforts, how Israel responded to what God was doing was critical. Jesus drew several contrasts between the way Israel responded and how the Gentiles had responded to what God was doing in the world. He pointed to the favorable response of the Ninevites when Jonah pointed to their unethical ways and their arrogance and called them to repentance. (12:41) Why was Israel not responsive in a similar manner when Jesus pointed out their failings?

Jesus also pointed to the ability of the queen of Sheba (12:42 and I Kings 10:1-13) to see divine wisdom in the wisdom of Solomon. This was in contrast to the people of God who were blind to a much clearer sign of the presence of God in Jesus' ministry. Earlier, in 11:22, the same unfavorable comparison was made between the people's response to Jesus' ministry and the arrogant, prideful people of Tyre and Sidon. In 11:24 the contrast was between Capernaum, Jesus' home town, and Sodom and Gomorrah. In 12:36 the religious leadership was warned of their accountability "on the day of judgment" for each word they had uttered. Now, in 12:41-42, Jesus says that the pagan Ninevites and the Queen of Sheba had been more responsive than the scribes and Pharisees had been to the Word of God. In each case, it was a Gentile response that compared favorably and reminded Israel of its vocation.

Persistence in Faith

Outsiders sometimes remind us of the true depth of faith.

In 15:21-28 Jesus had withdrawn into non-Jewish territory. A woman Matthew identifies as a Canaanite came to Jesus. In the Hebrew

Scriptures, the Canaanites were the hated rivals who lived in the Promised Land and who often seduced the faithful from the true worship of God. Why should Christ, or the Body of Christ, be concerned about those who represented everything the faithful were against and who often seduced believers from the faith? When this Canaanite woman asked Jesus for an act of compassion, Matthew described Jesus as not answering her a word (15:23). Though we do not know the reason for Jesus' silence, we know he did not try to get rid of her because, when the disciples came, they urged him to do just that. This pagan woman was offensive to the disciples. Jesus seemed to comply with the disciples' request and explained to the woman that he, whom she had already recognized as the Jewish Messiah by addressing him as Son of David, was sent only to the "lost sheep of the house of Israel." But she persisted by kneeling before him and saying, "Lord, help me." Jesus continued to respond to her in the form which the disciples would have expected. "It is not fair to take the children's food and throw it to the dogs." *Dogs* was a derogatory term that Israelites used for Gentiles or non-believers.

Like Amos who built on Israel's prejudice concerning other nations to convict Israel of its own failings (Amos 1:3-2:8), so by this dialogue Jesus led the disciples, who were subject to the temptation of self-righteous exclusivism, to the brink of their own self-understanding. As with the Pharisees and scribes who had studied God's law (15:1-20), now the disciples were tempted to use the law to excuse their lack of compassion for another human being.

Note the striking contrast between the woman's persistent faith and the skeptical questioning by the Pharisees and scribes who were supposed to be the elite of the people of God. While it was true that God had called Israel (the Church) to be God's special people, it was also true, as with the original call to Abram (Genesis 12:1-4), that by this specialness, the church was to be a blessing to all peoples. What the disciples failed to understand, the Canaanite woman understood. It was by her open vulnerability to God, and not by her defense of her national origin, that she received Christ's blessing. Instead of bristling when Jesus used a derogatory term about her, she persisted in her request.

As was true in the earlier story of the Roman Centurion's servant (8:5-13) referred to previously, so by the faith of this foreign woman, her daughter was healed. For Matthew's hearers, some of whom were probably of questionable origin and often the brunt of derogatory remarks, the reward of persistent faithfulness, rather than defensiveness, was good news.

Approaching the World

Jesus approached non-believers with compassion and without strings.

In 15:29-31 Jesus passed by the Sea of Galilee, went up into the hills and sat down. The phrasing is similar to the beginning of the Sermon on the Mount (5:1), only this time the crowd was largely Gentiles. The phrase, "and they praised the God of Israel" (15:31), would indicate this. It is interesting to contrast the way Jesus began with Israel (the church) and the way he began with the Gentiles (those outside the religious community). With the former, he began by teaching 5:1ff, but with the latter he responded first to their physical needs. There was healing within the religious community (9:1-8, 18-33), but it came in the context of faith and teaching. When the Gentiles came and placed the lame, maimed, blind, and dumb before Jesus, he healed them.

Jesus thus demonstrated that the bounty of God's blessing extended beyond the religious community and responded to the human need for wholeness and healing. The people gave glory to the God of Israel not because Jesus convinced them with his teachings or even used his healing powers to convict them of who he was, but because they experienced the good news of being made whole. It was when the Gentiles experienced

THE BOUNTY OF GOD'S BLESSING EXTENDED BEYOND THE RELIGIOUS COMMUNITY the blessing of Israel that they gave glory to the God of Israel. Jesus thus completed the promise of God given to Abram in Genesis 12:1-4.

Jesus did not try to convert them or pressure them to acknowledge him as Lord. Rather, Jesus responded to their need, and they freely responded by acknowledging the presence of God in what had happened. The task of the religious community thus becomes making manifest the glory of God by responding to the brokenness of the world with healing. It is when the world experiences such compassion without strings from the community of faith that they will wonder, because it is in such stark contrast to the way of the world. It is in the context of such freely given compassion that the world may freely choose to give glory to the God of Israel.

Meeting the World's Physical Needs

The mission of the church is not completed until the whole world is fed.

In 15:32-39 Matthew described the feeding of the four thousand, which is very similar to the feeding of the five thousand (14:13-21). The dissimilarities are worth examining. First, it was the Gentiles, rather than the Jews, who were fed. Second, it was Jesus, rather than the disciples, who took the initiative. Jesus said to his disciples,"I have compassion for the crowd, because they have been with me now for three days and have nothing to eat; and I do not want to send them away hungry, for they might faint on the way" (15:32). Third, the disciples had seven, rather than five, loaves. Fourth, there were seven baskets left over, rather than twelve. Finally, those who ate were four thousand men plus women and children, rather than five thousand plus women and children.

By including both stories, Matthew communicated the completeness of the church's mission. The five loaves of the first feeding and the seven loaves of the second make twelve, which indicates the full mission of the New Israel that will include both Jew and Gentile. In the second story, it was Jesus who took the initiative to leave no doubt as to the authenticity of the mission to Gentiles. It may also suggest that where the people of faith were slow to act, Jesus was already present and working.

The usual blessing before a Jewish meal, "Blessed art thou, 0 Lord our God, King of the World, who bringest forth bread from the earth," may well have been Jesus' blessing before each meal. Though Jesus came first to the Jews, he was unwilling to send the rest of the world away hungry, and neither should his disciples who make up the church. There were seven baskets left over, and seven is a biblical symbol of wholeness or completeness. The twelve baskets left over in the first feeding keep continuity with the twelve tribes of the original Israel that God continues to feed, but the seven baskets indicate Jesus' concern for the whole world. Both feedings were filled with new meaning by the Last Supper in which the Bread of Life was shared in the establishing of the New Covenant.

The church was thus commissioned to feed both its members and those outside its community because its mission is incomplete until all are fed. Though this certainly includes responsibility to feed people spiritually, it would be a mistake, in a time when hunger stalks

WHEN WE COMMIT WHAT WE HAVE TO CHRIST FOR THE SAKE OF THE WORLD, THERE WILL BE AMPLE LEFT OVER FOR THE COMMUNITY OF FAITH

the world, to overlook the fact that Jesus' compassion was raised by their physical hunger. If Jesus was unwilling to send them away hungry, then his church could hardly be faithful if they were willing to relax before the whole world is fed. The radical faith required is to believe, with the first disciples, that when we commit what we have to Christ for the sake of the world, there will be ample left over for the community of faith (twelve baskets) and the whole world (seven baskets).

Exploiting Foreigners

The church should not exploit the hunger of the world for its own profit.

In the cleansing of the Temple in 21:12-13, Jesus quoted a combination of Isaiah 56:7b and Jeremiah 7:11. The first quote reflected the universalism of Second Isaiah that found acceptable the sacrifice of foreigners who sought a right relation with God. The second reflected Jeremiah's denunciation of those who broke all the commandments with respect to right relationships and then thought that by regular attendance at Temple rituals they would be saved. Jesus made those quotes as he stood in the court of the Gentiles where the noise of the sellers prevented the Gentiles from worshiping and the exorbitant prices exploited the common worshiper.

The Roman coin, the common coin of the realm, bore an image of Caesar and an inscription attributing divinity to Caesar. Both the image and the inscription violated Jewish monotheism and, therefore, were unacceptable in Jewish worship. The moneychangers mediated this conflict between faith and society by allowing Gentiles and other pilgrims to exchange their coins for a Jewish coin which would be acceptable in temple worship. Like all those who seek to soften the conflict between faith and worldly pursuits, the money changers profited by exploiting the foreigners whose sacrifice God had found acceptable (Isaiah 56:7b).

The Accountability of Nations and Governments

While it is distinct from the church's responsibility, nations and governments also have a responsibility to which God hold's them accountable.

In 25:31-46 where Matthew describes the vision of judgment in which the sheep and the goats are separated, the universal nature of accountability is lifted up. Note that it is the nations, rather than individuals, that were gathered before the glorified Son of Man. Too often the import of this parable is missed because the emphasis is on individuals. For Matthew's congregation, who always lived in a tentative relationship with the governing powers of the nation, both because of their merchant status and their Christian faith, it was reassuring for them to recognize that the corporate power of nations also faced a judgment according to how it responded to the most needy in its midst. Though Israel, and later the church, was the bearer of the tradition by which believers could interpret what was happening in the world, the central issue was one of compassion for the needy. This was one of the commandments that Jesus commissioned them to teach the nation (28:20). In the same way that God heard the cry of distress of those who had been oppressed by the governing authorities in Egypt (Exodus 2:23-25), God also was aware and judged how other nations and peoples responded to the most needy within their midst. As Paul would discover on the road to Damascus (Acts 9:1-9), those who are persecuted have an advocate in the King (25:49).

It is important to realize that the sins of the nations noted here are sins of omission and not commission. In Matthew's version of the Good Samaritan, if a person is in need, the nation has a responsibility to reach out A NATION THAT FAILS TO BE COMPASSIONATE TO THE NEEDIEST AMONG THEM IS PREPARING ITSELF FOR ITS OWN DESTRUCTION and restore that person to wholeness. In Ezekiel 34 which undoubtedly provided the foundation for this parable, God judged the shepherds of Israel for feeding themselves and not feeding the sheep (Ezekiel 34:2-4). God also judged the strong sheep for taking advantage of the weak (Ezekiel 34:20-21), and, God would personally act to break the yoke that oppressed them (34:27). Matthew makes clear that God holds nations and governments accountable and will judge them.

If people care about their nation, they will do all within their power to urge it to be responsive to the hungry, the sick, the imprisoned, and so forth, because, despite its most righteous proclamations of innocence, a nation's survival depends upon its response to the needy.

Nations who follow the teachings of Christ by being responsive to the most needy in their midst will be the ones favored by God in their inheritance of a future. This does not suggest that nations should act like the church. As the righteous make clear by their response, they were not consciously serving Christ but only being compassionate. A nation that fails to be compassionate to the neediest among them is preparing itself for its own destruction. For a nation to "...go away into eternal punishment..." or "...into eternal life..." is to choose by its behavior whether it will participate in the rich, abundant life intended by God or whether it will destroy itself through its own selfishness.

Finding Release for the Oppressor

When the community of faith seeks to protect itself, it can easily become the oppressor rather than the bearer of good news for the world.

In 26:1-5 Matthew makes explicit the connection between the Passover and the coming crucifixion. In this connection one again sees the interplay between Israel and the nations. From the beginning of the Gospel, the question has been raised as to who was the real oppressor. When Herod tried to kill the child Jesus, it was Judea who became the oppressor and Egypt the place of refuge (2:13-15). This is a reversal of the original Exodus and raises the question of what type of Exodus is required when the community of faith is also the center of oppression? At the first Exodus, it was by the death of a lamb that the children of Israel were released from slavery (Exodus 12:13). Once more there would be a sacrifice, but this time the lamb would be Jesus.

If Abraham had to be willing to sacrifice his first born son Isaac, the child God had promised him, in order that in him all the nations of the world would be blessed (Genesis 22:15-18), then how much more was

God willing to sacrifice the first born of God that all the world might be released to its blessing? Those called to be the shepherds of Israel, the chief priests and elders, resisted this liberating activity of God by gathering to plot treachery against Jesus.

The drama of this conflict is heightened by recalling that Israel is God's first-born son (Exodus 4:22), and, as the prophet Hosea recounted, it was out of Egypt that God called his son (Hosea 11:14 and Matthew 2:15b). In Exodus it is recorded that God pitted God's first-born son, Israel, against the first-born of the oppressor in Egypt (Exodus 4:23). Now it was this same son, Israel, who had become the oppressor. In the first Passover, the first-born of the oppressors, the Egyptians, were sacrificed that the people of Israel might be released. The Passover was the time of release, but now, with Jesus, victory belonged not to the one who lived but the one who was willing to die.

The first Exodus was brought about by God's judgment of the oppressor that resulted in the suffering and death of their first born, their heirs apparent. The new Exodus, a time which would usher in a whole new world, was to come about through overcoming the reality of death. God allowed God's son to be crucified that the oppressor might find release. The old world was moved to action by the fear of the pain of death. The new world would find release through the hope of the possibilities in a new life.

Whenever the community of faith becomes more concerned about preserving its own life than in responding to the needs of the oppressed, it becomes the oppressor rather than the bearer of life.

Like Abraham, the son of God (Israel or Jesus?) had to be willing to sacrifice all to God before the world could receive its blessing. For the moment, the leaders of Israel were so caught up in their schemes to protect themselves that they failed to experience release into new life. In Israel's story it was made clear that even those once released from oppression and adopted as full children of God were not immune from becoming the new oppressors. For Matthew's congregation, which had found new release in Jesus, and for the rather uneven history of the church, it was a cogent warning.

Experiencing Truth in the Heart of Terror

God reconciles the polarities of our world by participating in and transforming that which we might initially judge as evil.

Having celebrated the Passover meal together, Jesus and his disciples went out to the Mount of Olives. In the book of the prophet Ezekiel, the Son of Man was shown that because of the idolatry of the city (Ezekiel 8:15-18) and the sins of its leaders (Ezekiel 11:1-13), the glory of God departed Jerusalem and stood on the Mount of Olives (Ezekiel 11:23) in order to draw the faithful to God and reestablish a faithful Israel. Jesus, having sung the traditional Passover hymn, perhaps Psalms 114 that recalled the Exodus event, made that same journey to the Mount of Olives. Symbolically the "glory of God" had again departed from Jerusalem because of the corruption of the city and its leaders? The "glory of God" again stood on the Mount of Olives in order to draw the faithful from all the countries together in a purified Israel (Ezekiel 11:17ff).

When Jesus reached the Mount of Olives, he warned his disciples against too easy an interpretation of the symbolism of his movements. He told them that they, too, would be scandalized by the events of the night. To help them understand, he quoted from Zechariah 13:7, "Strike the shepherd, that the sheep may be scattered." Consider the scandal of Jesus suggesting that God would be a participant in the evil of the night. It would be far easier to keep God in the heavens and see the betrayal and crucifixion as a result of evil triumphing over good. But, said Jesus, it would be God who would participate in the night of betrayal; it would be God who would strike the shepherd. The scandal of believing that

God participated in such evil would overwhelm his disciples because they still saw Jesus as being rescued by God at the last moment.

Zechariah's prophecy pictured God standing on the Mount of Olives and reconciling the polarities of the world (Zechariah 14:6-8) under the one rule of God (Zechariah 14:9). The disciples still anticipated this happening by means of a mighty display of divine power. Jesus recognized, however, that it would begin to happen through the betrayal and crucifixion. God's faithfulness would first be experienced in Galilee--the Galilee of the Gentiles (4:15) where Jew and Gentile met. It was there that the scandalized disciples would meet the resurrected Christ and begin to recognize the left hand of God, God's ability to transform evil and defeat, as being part of God's reconciling purpose.

Impetuous Peter, the rock upon which the community of faith was founded (16:18), and, therefore, the church's representative in these conversations, boasted that he had grasped the full truth of what was about to happen and would not be scandalized. Jesus recognized that God's truth was not something grasped by the intellect but rather something experienced in the heart of terror, so he insisted that Peter would be so affronted by the ease with which evil seemed to triumph in the coming events that he would disavow his relationship with Jesus three times in one night. Peter insisted, as did the rest of the disciples, that his mind and heart were in the same place, and he would remain faithful even if it meant his death.

> JESUS RECOGNIZED THAT GOD'S TRUTH WAS NOT SOMETHING GRASPED BY THE INTELLECT BUT RATHER SOMETHING EXPERIENCED IN THE HEART OF TERROR

In early Israel, Satan was seen as the adversary who challenged but nevertheless was a servant (son) of God (Job 1:6ff) who effected God's purpose. Sometimes the name Satan and God would be interchanged in the same story—see 2 Samuel 24:1 and 1 Chronicles 21:1. In all cases, Satan was never beyond the control of God (Zechariah 3:1-2). The judgment or wrath of God never triumphed over the redeeming purpose of God, yet it was and continues to be difficult for Christians to both trust and perceive God actually participating in evil in order to transform it for a greater good. For Jesus, the tension between the power of evil and his trust in the goodness of God became almost unbearable (27:46). In recounting the story, Matthew wanted the continuing community of faith to know that even denial was not irredeemable. For Matthew's congregation who were constantly experiencing the tension between the temptations of the mercantile world and the faithful response, this was good news. Even current day denials can be a context for the redemptive process of God.

The Left Hand of God

The freedom of God transcends that which the religious community deems good or faithful.

When Judas was struck by the implications of his sinful betrayal, (27:3-10) he tried to return the money to the chief priests. The priests, who have responsibility to offer a ritual cleansing of sins (Deuteronomy 21:5-9), refused to exercise that role, thus leaving Judas without hope. The priests became worthless shepherds who deserted their flock (Zechariah 11:17).

The Zechariah reference around which Matthew interpreted these actions of Judas (Zechariah 11:1-17) also included thirty pieces of silver that bought betrayal and came from the Temple treasury. Therefore, from Matthew's perspective, God was again guiding a worthless shepherd, Judas, as part of God's redemptive purpose. The casting of the thirty pieces of silver into the Temple, perhaps according to the Greek toward the Holy of Holies, was an indictment of the failure of Temple and its leaders, whose exploitation of the people was destroying the community. The implication was that, though Judas' act was evil in a shadowy sort of way, it reflected the Left Hand of God present in the events which were leading toward the cross.

The chief priests were conscious at some level of both their guilt and the symbolic annulment of the covenant between the religious structure purporting to represent Israel and God through the thirty pieces of silver cast into the Temple (Zechariah 11:13-14). They tried to perform their own symbolic act. As did Jeremiah at the time of the destruction of Jerusalem (Jeremiah 32:9-15), they purchased a field as a sign of future hope in God's promise. They bought what is called the "potters field," perhaps referring to the image of God as potter in Jeremiah 18:1-6, but designated it for the burial of foreigners. For Matthew this act also foreshadowed God's remolding Israel to include those formerly called foreigners.

The whole passage (Matthew 27:1-10) speaks of the freedom of God to annul promises made to those who prove faithless and yet work through the betrayer's hands to effect a higher purpose. For Israel, and later the church that presumed to bear the faith of Israel,

> GOD CAN WORK THROUGH THE BETRAYER'S HAND TO CREATE THE EVENTS WHICH LEAD TO SALVATION.

there was both warning and hope. God punishes in order to save. The faithless need to be aware that, though the fulfillment of God's intentions was not dependent on their faithfulness, God was free to restructure the source through which the promise was fulfilled. God can work through the betrayer's hand to create the events which lead to that salvation.

God's Use of Strangers

The faithful must pay attention to those who do not share their faith if they are to hear the full truth of God.

In 27:19 there was a brief incident reported which continued to emphasize Matthew's theme of God's work through pagans in revealing the truth which the faithful refuse to acknowledge. As was true with the Magi in 2:12, God communicated with Pilate's wife in a dream. Though the Sanhedrin refused to recognize Jesus for who he truly was, through a dream God communicated to Pilate's wife that Jesus was a righteous man. Such knowledge brought only partial understanding. It would still require the keepers of the Scriptures to recognize the full significance of Jesus, but until they were willing to do so, God continued to display the freedom to reveal such truth through unexpected channels.

In 27:32, it was a stranger and foreigner who fulfilled the role that should have been fulfilled by one of the faithful. It was Simon of Cyrene who was pressed into service to help Jesus carry the cross. Neither his accusers nor his followers, both drawn from the community of faith, aided Jesus in that last painful journey. So God continued to exercise freedom in the drama that was being acted out, and thus revealed the importance of the foreigner in bearing the burden of truth when the faithful were not prepared to do so. God's plan to save the world did not depend on the people of faith; the people of faith depended upon God's plan to save the world. But it was the world, not just a particular people, which was the focus of God's activity.

Removing the Last Barrier

Gentiles, or people not of our faith, are the first to recognize Jesus at his birth and among the last to recognize him at his death.

In 27:51-54 when Jesus had yielded up his spirit to God, no longer clinging even to his last breath as a means of maintaining some control over his response to events, the curtain which separated the Holy of Holies from the rest of the Temple was split in two. By such total commitment to the "will of God," even in the face of evil that caused Jesus to experience a deep gulf between his perceptions of reality and the presence of God, the last barrier between God and humanity was removed. Previously, access to God had been blocked by a misunderstanding that God could be sought only by the pure and undefiled and religious law viewed death as unclean (Leviticus 21:11). But clearly, the truth of God was present even in the touch of death.

The whole earth was shaken by this open access to God's presence. Verse 52 echoes Ezekiel 37, especially verses 12 and 13. In that chapter Ezekiel was commanded to announce God's breathing life into a valley of dry bones, and then it was explained that this resurrection and restoration to life of these dry bones was symbolic of what God would do for Israel. The breath that finally animated the reassembled bones to life was from God. For Matthew it was by Jesus' complete submission to the will of God that God's spirit or breath gave life to the community of God's kingdom. This new community had open access to God and experienced a triumph over death.

All that had blocked access to God, whether the defilement of death or even a racial separateness, was suddenly overcome. Even the Gentile centurion and other soldiers who were assigned the death watch over those who were crucified were so moved by the events that they were filled with awe. Even from their limited background, they were able to declare, "Truly this man was God's Son!" (27:54). In this way the Gospel comes full circle from the Gentile wise men (2:1-12) who recognized Jesus at birth to the Roman soldiers who recognized him at death. As was said in Ephesians 2:11-22, "...you who once were far off have been brought near by the blood of Christ." By Jesus' consistent focus on the "will of God," the dividing walls were broken down.

For Matthew's congregation, who in their work as urban merchants often had to become involved with actions that Jewish law declared to be unclean, this message of triumph was indeed good news. The message also shifted the focus of life from trying to protect oneself and avoiding the experience of evil to trying to discover the presence of God in even the darkest of circumstances. The horizon of God's presence was thus broadened to include even the most tragic of situations. It was the entire world, and not just some religious corner within it, that became the arena in which people can encounter the presence of God.

In some senses, the holy was profaned so that the profane might be made holy.

CHAPTER 3

RESPONSE TO A WORLD
DIVIDED INTO MALE AND FEMALE

I do not know whether anyone has ever suggested that Matthew was written by a female; but if this Gospel was written by a male, it was a male who had experienced a transformation that made him extraordinarily sensitive to the dignity of women in a society with a firm pattern of patriarchy.

The Scandalous Women

If there was ever evidence of the power of Christ to transform lives well in advance of the progress of society, it is certainly found in the Gospel of Matthew.

The author of the Gospel consistently challenges the presuppositions of that patriarchal society in a bold and forthright manner. The first clue to Matthew's radical perspective with respect to women is found in the genealogical table of the ancestry of Jesus. Unlike most genealogical tables, which would have been used by the elite to substantiate their place in society, Matthew includes women in the list. To mention women in a Jewish genealogy was very unusual because the Jews believed the bloodline was solely determined by the male. To add to the surprise, as was mentioned in Chapter 2, the first woman to be mentioned, Tamar, was a foreigner. The torrid story of Judah and Tamar, which may well be symbolic of the Jewish (Judah) relationship with other nations (Tamar), suggested that at times God went to extraordinary lengths to call God's people back to faithfulness.

In verse 5 two more women of foreign origin are mentioned. The first is Rahab, the prostitute who hid Joshua's spies in preparation for the Israelite invasion of the land (Joshua 2). The second is Ruth, a Moabitess, whose nation was hated by Jews, who through her cunning and loyalty to her Jewish mother-in-law, Naomi, won the love of Boaz, a Jew.

Lest we forget the context, Matthew emphasized that Solomon was the result of David's adulterous affair with Bathsheba, the wife of Uriah, one of David's soldiers. The shameful story, (2 Samuel 11-12), told how great King David had an affair with the wife of one of his soldiers. When she became pregnant, David was perfectly willing to return her to Uriah, her husband, if he could cover up his act. When that became impossible because this Hittite soldier was more loyal to the laws of the day than was David, David arranged to have Uriah killed in order to protect the king's reputation.

From these four women—one a prostitute, one who seduced her father-in-law, one who exhibited loyalty and cunning, and one who was an adulteress—came the line that was to produce the child Jesus. The fifth woman mentioned, Mary, also raises a question. If the bloodline was traced through males and Joseph was not the father of the child Jesus, then who was?

> FROM FOUR WOMEN—ONE A PROSTITUTE, ONE WHO SEDUCED HER FATHER-IN-LAW, ONE WHO EXHIBITED LOYALTY AND CUNNING, AND ONE WHO WAS AN ADULTERESS—CAME THE LINE THAT WAS TO PRODUCE THE CHILD JESUS.

Does Matthew suggest that if one wants to know the true origin of Jesus and Jesus' true significance, then one needs to pay attention to women and not just men? By the ethical standards of the day, Mary's condition of birth was a scandal covered up only by the compassion of Joseph. Yet if one reflects on the genealogical table, it was often at the point of scandal, where others might dismiss someone in righteous judgment, that one needed to look most carefully for the sign of God's presence.

To dismiss Mary as an immoral woman, which by all appearances she was, would block out the possibility of hearing God's word as expressed through Mary and her child. The name of this child was Jesus, which came from the same Hebrew root as the name Joshua, meaning "God saves." The message in Jesus was the same as that throughout Hebrew history: it is God, not our moral sensibilities, who saves, and God alone.

A Woman Bears the Word of God

God chooses a woman to bear the word of God to a world blinded by its positions of privilege and power.

The birth fulfills Isaiah's prophesy (7:1-15): "Behold a virgin shall conceive and bear a son, and his name shall be called Emmanuel (which means, God with us)." This quote refers to a time when Ahaz and the city of Jerusalem were being attacked by a coalition of Syria and the northern kingdom of Israel. Isaiah was trying to convince Ahaz that he should place his trust in God, rather than in a military alliance with the superpower Assyria. When Ahaz refused, Isaiah said that God would provide a sign in the form of a young woman who would bear a son who would be called Emmanuel. When Ahaz, in a position of power, refused to be responsive to the word of God, it was a woman who bore a sign of God's presence. Matthew saw that same prophetic word being fulfilled again. A woman was able to bear the authentic message of God's word to a society of privileged men who were blinded by their positions. Again, as with Ahaz, it was those in positions of power in society that were unable to place their trust in God and, therefore, missed the sign of God's presence. It was only Joseph, who obeyed God by responding to Mary and her needs, rather than defending his "rights," who contributed to the fulfillment of God's purpose.

Feminine Images of God

Scripture consistently reveals that God has used women to reveal a radical new departure that God was introducing in our world.

In addition to the image of a woman being the bearer of the Word of God to a world that trusted in its own wisdom more than it trusted in God, Matthew drew on three feminine images of God used by three separate prophets in an attempt to explain this radical thing which God had done. First, in 2:6 when the Magi came to inquire as to the location of the birth of the new Messiah, Matthew quoted from Micah 5:2, the context of which is that of the prophet creating a metaphor of faith from Israel's experience of defeat under Saul. Saul had been humiliated by the Philistines in battle, yet God drew David out of the weakest clan in Judah to restore and deliver Israel. Victory, said Micah, belonged not to the strong or mighty but to the faithful, who understood that fears and even defeats can be God's labor pains as she gives birth to new hope (Micah 5:3). By reference to this feminine image of God giving birth in midst of pain, together with the pagan display of faithfulness by the Magi even at great risk to themselves, Matthew prepared his hearers for this radically new experience of faith. The message to Matthew's hearers challenged the belief that pain, defeat, or weakness was necessarily a barrier to the fulfillment of God's purpose.

Second, the apparent power of Herod demonstrated in the quick flight of Joseph, Mary, and Jesus into Egypt prompted Matthew to quote Hosea 11:1, "Out of Egypt have I called my son." Hosea made reference to Exodus 4:22 in which God claimed Israel as God's first-born son. For Matthew, who saw Jesus as the living fulfillment of Israel and, therefore, God's first born son, this was significant in that the passage in Hosea from which the quote was drawn developed the tension now evident between the historical Israel and Jesus. Though Hosea saw God as having called Israel out of Egypt, Hosea also recorded Israel's continual rebellion against the purposes of God. Therefore, the fact that "all Jerusalem" as well as Herod were frightened by the announcement of Christ's birth (2:3) was but additional evidence of the continual rebellion of the people of Israel against the fulfillment of their calling. A further reading of the context of the quote reveals that Matthew used a third feminine image to expose this radically new departure that God was introducing into the world. Hosea saw God's relationship to Israel as that of a compassionate mother who "...led them with cords of human kindness, with bands of love. I was to them like those who lift infants to their cheeks. I bent down to them and fed them" (11:4).

In 1:23 Matthew quoted Isaiah as describing a woman who gave birth as a sign of God's presence in the face of the king's refusal to recognize the trustworthiness of God. In 2:6 Matthew quoted Micah, who saw the painful humiliation of the people of Israel as divine labor pains which would issue in the birth of new hope. In Matthew 2:16-23, it is also made clear that God is not a dispassionate observer of events, but is compassionately involved like a mother who gives birth to her children, then makes every effort to nurture them and protect them from harm.

In this passage the political reaction to the birth of the Prince of Peace is one of furious rage. Herod immediately ordered the killing of all male children in Bethlehem and the surrounding region who were two years old or under. Such an atrocity immediately recalls a parallel event in Exodus 1:15-2:10 in which the Pharaoh was threatened by the growth in number of the Israelites and ordered all male children killed at birth. Exodus 4:22 reminds us that this also was the killing of the child of God. In

> MATTHEW WAS SAYING THAT WHILE THE WORLD WAS WATCHING THE RANTING AND RAVING OF THE MEN IN POWER, IF YOU WANTED TO KNOW WHAT GOD WAS DOING, "WATCH THE WOMEN!"

Exodus God worked through the faith of women to preserve Israel: first the mid-wives (Exodus 1:17), then a mother and her daughter (Exodus 2:2-4), and finally the Pharaoh's own daughter (Exodus 2:5-6). It is as if Matthew was saying that while the world was watching the ranting and raving of the men in power, to know what God was doing, "watch the women!"

The world's violence needs to be protested by the Rachel in each of us that refuses to be consoled in the face of evil. But for Matthew, such violence does not end in protest. God is seen in Jesus' reaching into the world of violence and giving birth to new hope.

The fourth prophet Matthew quoted was Jeremiah and, again it was a feminine image that was used. The quote was from Jeremiah 31:15-22 but referred back to the story of Rachel and Leah in Genesis 29:31-30:21. Rachel was the favorite wife of Jacob, but she was barren, while her sister Leah and a couple of maids produced child after child. The Jewish people, as they suffered defeat and exile, identified with Rachel. What good was it to be the favored one if life was always dealing you bad blows? Finally, Rachel bore a child named Joseph and was soon pregnant again. But the second birth was too strenuous for Rachel and, as life was ebbing from her, she named him Benoni--son of my sorrows, her unanswered protest hurled out at the universe against the injustice of it all. Death at birth seemed to contradict the very promise of God.

Rachel was buried at Rama, and the tradition grew that the spirit of Rachel, the ancestress of Israel, continued to mourn and protest the fate of chosen Israel whose sorrowful experience seemed to contradict the very promise of God. When the prophet Jeremiah faced the defeat and destruction of the nation of Israel, he referred to the tradition of Rachel crying out in protest at the death of her children Israel. It was the cry of a mother's grief that refused consolation, refused to be comfortable with the contradictions in life.

Rachel's cry was a metaphor for God's mourning. The mother in God resonated with mother Rachel, " 'Is Ephraim my dear son? Is he the child I delight in? As often as I speak against him, I still remember him. Therefore I am deeply moved for him; I will surely have mercy on him,' says the Lord" (Jeremiah 31:20). Out of God's creative power, she gave birth to a *new creation*. So radical is the break from normal that everything was reversed. Ephraim, the son of God in verse 20 of Jeremiah 31, was described as virgin Israel in verse 21, "For the Lord has created a new thing on the earth: a woman encompasses (or protects RSV) a man" (Jeremiah 31:22). Matthew completed the fulfillment of this prophesy in 26:6-13.

For Matthew, Jeremiah's promise of a new creation finds fulfillment in the birth of Jesus that takes place in the midst of the fratricidal tendencies of humanity. The violence of the world cannot and should not be justified. To give an explanation for such violence would be to justify it, so it remains unexplained--hanging like Rachel's protest.

Watch the Women

It was in the women's response to Jesus that the power of Jesus to set one free from that which oppressed and crippled one in society was made evident.

In 8:14-17 Matthew briefly described Jesus' healing of Peter's mother-in-law. Unlike all other healings by Jesus that the Gospel records, this one described Jesus taking the initiative. In the Jewish patriarchal society, at marriage the wife left her family and became part of her husband's family. The fact that Peter's mother-in-law was in Peter's house suggested a very unusual circumstance. Apparently not only was her husband dead, but also the family from which Peter's wife came would not or could not care for her. Further, her health was such that she could not even be of service. A widowed mother-in-law would have no claim upon her daughter's married family, and her illness would prevent her from being anything but a burden.

It was to this most vulnerable of people that Jesus took the initiative to reach out in healing. When she was healed, she rose and served Jesus. By Jesus' touch, she regained her dignity and acted out her recognition that Jesus was Lord. Again Matthew seemed to suggest "Watch the women!"

Sometimes one can allow one's position or even respect for religious tradition to block our access to the healing love of God.

Following completion of the Sermon on the Mount, Matthew described ten miraculous actions that revealed how Jesus exercised authority in relationship to the rest of the world. The seventh and eighth of those acts involved women, continuing Matthew's theme of watching the women for signs of the new creation (9:18-26). The seventh mighty act started out to be the experience of resurrection, but it was interrupted by a woman who was separated from the community by her condition of bleeding; a condition that by Old Testament laws rendered her unclean (Leviticus 15:25-33). Seven is a Biblical symbol of wholeness, and the seventh mighty act overcame the division between cleanness and uncleanness and reunited the woman to the community.

The eighth act then became the first act of the new beginning which was new life. Where the law separated, faith made whole. Where death destroyed, faith gave new life. Each of these two incidents of Jesus' healing touch was described briefly by Matthew. Each was Jesus' response to an initial act of faith by someone else. Each reflected evidence of the new reality created by the authority of Jesus.

First, a ruler of the synagogue asked on behalf of his daughter, "My daughter has just died, but come and lay your hand on her, and she will live"(9:18). The second was a woman who has suffered from a hemorrhage for twelve years. Mark reported she had gone from physician to physician and spent all her money without finding a cure. Each had ample evidence to believe no one could help—the one because who can alter the finality of death; the other because she had sought help many times before without success.

Both had reason to believe that reaching out to Jesus involved great risk to them personally. The ruler of the synagogue had a position to protect. Being made a fool by a questionable rabbi would not do any good for him or the people of the synagogue for whom he was responsible. When Jesus approached the ruler's home, the people ridiculed the thought that Jesus could help. The fact that the leader asked Jesus to do what only God could do opened him to ridicule as well, but his love for his daughter was so strong that he dared to take the risk.

For the woman, who was bleeding, to reach out and touch a rabbi would render him unclean as well and most likely incur his rebuke rather than his compassion. The tassels on his robe that she sought to touch were a reminder to obey the commandments (Numbers 15:37-41) not to deliberately flaunt them. Yet her need was so great that she dared risk rebuke and violation of the law in order to touch the mercy of God. Symbolically, both the act that fulfilled the old creation and that which initiated the new creation resulted from taking a risk in the face of what appeared to be insolvable problems. Neither one's standing in life nor accepted religious standards were to prevent the discovery that God responds to both love of another and to deeply felt need.

The Influence that Permeates

The kingdom of heaven is characterized as an influence that permeates rather than a force that dominates.

In 13:33 Matthew quoted Jesus as suggesting the Kingdom of Heaven was like a woman who hid leaven in three measures of meal until it was all leavened. Leaven permeates the larger mass, yet is not visible in the process. Since the leaven was hidden in the meal by the woman, there may be a prophetic warning against anyone concluding that he or she knows where the Word of God is at work and where it is not. The source of leaven and even apparently the kneading by which it was worked into the meal was from outside the meal. There is no room here for taking pride in one's own power and goodness.

Presuming that as a child Jesus watched his mother make bread, he may well have been aware of the importance of the environment in which the prepared dough was placed. If the atmosphere was too cold, the yeast would not cause the dough to rise. Thus, though the source of God's leaven is beyond us, the atmosphere we create may block

> THOUGH THE SOURCE OF GOD'S LEAVEN IS BEYOND US, THE ATMOSPHERE WE CREATE MAY BLOCK OR ACTIVATE THE PROCESS OF THE YEAST PERMEATING OUR LIVES OR THE LIFE OF A CONGREGATION.

or activate the process of the yeast permeating our lives or the life of a congregation.

This image shatters our usual understanding of how kingdoms rule and how real change occurs. The gifts of the Spirit–such as joy, truth, love, peace, and so forth–are planted in us by God, like a woman plants leaven in meal, ready to permeate one's whole character if the right environment is created. Yet the actual working of these gifts as they transform one's life and world remains a mystery beyond human control.

The story of the Canaanite woman in 15:21-28 has been examined in Chapter 2. It should be noted, however, that as will be true in 26:6-13, it was a woman of questionable origin, in this case a pagan, whose insight into the true significance of Jesus was contrasted with the lack of insight of his most trusted male disciples. Is Matthew suggesting that though the twelve male disciples expressed the continuity of Israel, to truly receive the blessings of God, one must be open to the discontinuity expressed through the vulnerable and persistent request of one who stood outside of both the faith parameters and the patriarchal parameters of Israel?

The Foundation of the Church

The foundation of the church includes a blending of the masculine and the feminine.

In 16:16-20 Jesus heard Simon confess his belief that Jesus was the Christ, the son of the living God. Jesus' response was to pronounce God's blessing on Simon, "Blessed are you, Simon son of Jonah," and to give him a name reflective of his new call, "You are Peter." Like Saul, who also received a new name reflective of his call, there was a recognition that Simon Peter's new understanding was neither the result of intellectual insight, nor of human loyalty to the person of Jesus, "For flesh and blood has not revealed this to you..." Faith must always be received with humility in response to an act of grace and can never be a source of human pride.

"...You are Peter (Petros), and on this rock (Petra), I will build my church." The name Peter (Petros) was a masculine word meaning stone. The word used for rock, Petra, was feminine. Though the pun was surely intended, the change in gender may be more than recognition that Peter was a man. That which inspired Peter was the Holy Spirit, which in Greek is also feminine. The church (feminine) may well be founded on one's response to the grace offered by God that here includes a blending of the masculine (Peter) and the Spirit (feminine).

The church was surely not founded on Peter's character, which proved wanting almost immediately (16:22-23). That which the powers of death, or as in Greek, "the gates of Hades," could not prevail against, was that which had its origin and foundation in the divine initiative rather than in human character.

Like Jesus, the church as the Body of Christ can not be imprisoned or destroyed by death, so it is free to respond in faith to God.

"I will give you the keys of the kingdom of heaven, and whatever you bind on earth will be bound in heaven..." (16:19). The keys of the kingdom were clearly a sign of authority but not the authority that came from personal power. The parallel in Isaiah 22:20ff and again in Revelation 3:7 clearly indicate that this authority was based on God's ultimate faithfulness and not on the exercise of personal power. In Isaiah, the current status of the one offered the keys, Eliakim, from the viewpoint of the world, was one of weakness. His strength was only in his trust in one who would be faithful to him despite all logic drawn from current conditions. In Revelation, it was the church in Philadelphia whose power was little (Revelation 3:8).

The key is to understand "in whom one can really trust." This can unlock or open one to the eternal. The authority given Peter, the pebble who by his response reflected a cornerstone, was not to *determine* but to *reflect* the eternal because, by faith, he (she--the church) was set free of the concern for death that normally binds us. One who no longer was bound by death, in any of its forms, was truly set free to reflect eternal truths to a world that still walked in darkness.

Through Death to Life

The church, especially when it experiences the power of faith given to it, is tempted to cling to and seek to control that faith as a possession, rather than follow it as a radical alternative to the world view that now oppresses both the church and the world.

Peter's recognition of Jesus as the Christ marked a turning point in the Gospel. Jesus, in 16:21-23, began to try to include his disciples in an awareness of the new reality inaugurated by his presence. What began in Jesus, the Christ, was not another reform movement, but a totally new beginning, a new birth, that emerged out of death. Matthew had seen in the birth of Jesus (2:18) the fulfillment of what Jeremiah saw in the fall of Judah (Jeremiah 31:15ff): that new birth emerges out of genuine grief. Jeremiah had used the image of Rachel's unconsoled grieving for her children to show how God grieved for her people as judgment fell on them and they were taken into exile. Yet the pain was necessary because the old pattern of life, which had been so well protected and justified, had to be broken before the people could recognize that God was giving them a totally new hope. Jesus told his disciples that the yearning for the restoration of Israel–which was represented by the Sanhedrin, the elders, chief priests, and scribes who guide and protect Israel–would be shattered by Israel's leader's rejection of the very one God sent. Only then could the disciples be open to the new thing that God was doing in their midst.

Jesus recognized that only as his disciples passed through the experience of death to hope would they discover the alternative reality which he represented. The church would be

> THE CHURCH IS CONSTANTLY FACING THE CHOICE BETWEEN SURVIVAL AND FAITHFULNESS.

constantly facing the choice between survival and faithfulness. Both Old Israel and New Israel must discover again that God's blessings in life are given, not earned; appreciated, not possessed.

Women in God's New Reality

Women are created in the image of God. To deny their full humanity is to turn your back on the revelation of God reflected in their lives.

A glimpse of that new reality could be seen in Jesus' response to a challenge by the Sadducees in 22:23-33. Through making accommodations with their imperial rulers and with the thought process of their contemporary world, the Sadducees had become the aristocrats of the priestly families (Acts 5:17). They were neither interested in nor looking for a time when God would intervene and change things, because they prospered so richly from the way things were. Not feeling deprived in this world, they disparaged any belief in the resurrection, and it was this idea with which they sought to trap Jesus. The law upon which they based their challenge was from Deuteronomy 25:5-10: "When brothers reside together, and one of them dies and has no son, the wife of the deceased shall not be married outside the family to a stranger. Her husband's brother shall go in to her, taking her in marriage . . ." The original purpose of the law was to protect the land and means of livelihood that had been allotted to each family when the line of inheritance was endangered due to the lack of a son. It proposed that if a married man died without a son as heir, it was the obligation of his brother to have a son by his dead brother's wife, and thus produce an heir for him. The irony of their question was that most families had already lost their family allotment of land to the wealthy, such as the Sadducees, who had secured land through foreclosure on bad debts. But none of this mattered because the Sadducees' real intention was to use the ancient law as a means of entrapping Jesus in what they perceived as the illogic of the idea of the resurrection.

For the Sadducees it was the presuppositions contained in their hypothetical situation of a woman who had been married to seven brothers that tripped them up. They assumed that by reason of marriage a woman became the possession of a man and, if seven had "had her," to whom would she belong or "be wife?" Jesus' response was that in the resurrection she belonged to no one, but rather was like a messenger of God or angel in her own right. By such a response, Jesus declared that it was not God's intention that women should be considered property in any fashion.

In an agrarian society, it was in the upper-class elite that women were most likely to be seen as a possession rather than a person, because in the lower classes, survival dictated that women

> IT WAS NOT GOD'S INTENTION THAT WOMEN SHOULD BE CONSIDERED PROPERTY IN ANY FASHION

and men work as partners. Jesus was directly challenging any thought of women being anything other than human beings created in the image of God, who in the resurrection, would more perfectly reflect that image like a messenger (angel) reflects the message or intent of the sender. The affluent Sadducees had accommodated themselves to the world, as illustrated by their attitude towards women, and had, therefore, blinded themselves to the revelation of God.

Midwives of a New Age

Can we see a reflection of the work of God in the birth process of women?

In 23:37 at the conclusion of Jesus' funeral lament for Jerusalem (see Chapter 5), having laid symbolic claim to being representative of the glory of God, Jesus used the feminine image of a mother hen's care for her brood to represent God's love for Jerusalem. It was as if Jesus was saying that the legalism and hypocrisy of the religious leaders, which had become enmeshed in the images of patriarchy, must be broken open by creative new images if the rebirth of faith was to take place.

As described in Chapter 2, Matthew saw Jesus' departure from Jerusalem to the Mount of Olives as a reenactment of Ezekiel's picture of God's glory leaving the Temple and moving to the Mount of Olives east of the city (Ezekiel 11:23). Continuing that theme of Ezekiel, the disciples knew that God would reject the shepherds or religious leaders who had failed in their care for their sheep, and that God would personally intervene to rescue the sheep or the people (Ezekiel 34). So the disciples came to the "departed glory" which sat on the Mount of Olives, and asked him about the parousia–the arrival of the time when God would defeat evil and restore wholeness to the creation, the time when the glory of the Lord would return to God's temple (Ezekiel 43:2-5).

The further Israel was removed from the time of its nationhood and the greater the powers like the Roman Empire controlled the people's lives, the more apocalyptic their speculation became. Because they could not believe that God would abandon them, the idea of the Messiah changed from the expectation of a new earthly leader to that of a supernatural figure who would command God's army and overthrow the wicked who oppressed them. The battle scene pictured by Ezekiel was of great hordes of the wicked (Ezekiel 38:9), who would array themselves against the faithful with seemingly invincible power. At that moment, when evil did its worst to them, God would personally summon every kind of terror and all the natural forces to utterly defeat the forces of evil, thus vindicating the holiness of God (Ezekiel 38:17-23).

In the book of Daniel, God gave dominion of the restored kingdom to "one like a son of man" (Daniel 7:13 NRSV footnote). The disciples were joining in this "end time speculation," having picked up the clear allusions to the prophet Ezekiel in Jesus' words and actions and wanted to know when these events might occur. Jesus warned them against speculation that made one susceptible to false messiahs and the misreading of historical events.

Every generation believes that its disasters (wars, earthquakes, and famines) are so evil that God will choose that particular age to intervene personally and defeat evil. As with the Temple, such a reading of the signs is a form of restricting God's freedom and, therefore, questioning whether God or event is Lord. If events are Lord, then the events will eventually force God's intervention; but if God is Lord, then God will choose.

Though each generation thinks the suffering and the evil around it are the worst, history would indicate that God has continually exercised the divine freedom to work through such events in order to effect the divine purpose. Again Jesus drew upon a feminine image to instruct his disciples as to the meaning of the events which they were experiencing. Such sufferings were not a sign that evil was reaching a level that would force God to intervene, but rather were the "birth-pangs of the new age" (24:8). God was neither being forced to act nor indifferent to such events, but rather God was using them like a woman in labor because of the life that was to come. The task of the disciples was to be midwives who refused to obey the forces of death and, therefore, enabled the new life that God intended to emerge (Exodus 1:17).

In the years that followed Jesus' death, there was much speculation as to his immediate return and the end of the age. In these verses Matthew cautioned his hearers that such speculation about the end of the world could divert their attention from the responsibility of midwifery to which they (and we) were called.

Preparation for Resistance

Though one can waste energy by needless speculation about the end time, Matthew also warned his readers in 24:9-14 that one should not be naive about the tension that would exist between those who hold on to the old age and those who seek to assist in the birth of the new age.

Violent resistance to the new age is foreshadowed by Matthew all through the Gospel beginning with the reaction of Herod and Jerusalem when news first reached them of Jesus' birth (2:3 and 2:16). As Christianity reached out beyond Israel, which Matthew's hearers were experiencing, that same resistance would continue to be confronted in other nations as well.

The "new age," which was inaugurated by Jesus, was not just an individual spiritual journey, but stood as a basic challenge to the very structures by which nations derived their support. Jesus was not anti-institutional, but he was clear that God was Lord of such principalities and that their existence could be justified only to the degree that they aided in the fulfillment of God's intent. When institutions became forces that tempted people to violate the demands of social justice and mercy, such institutions became demonic. But such principalities or institutions did

THE GOSPEL OF LOVE WOULD NOT ALWAYS BE RECEIVED LOVINGLY BY THOSE WHOSE EXISTENCE WAS BASED ON FEAR AND GREED not die easily. The old world, which saw religion as supportive of their accommodations with *necessary inequities* in society, would be angry with those of the new creation, who challenged the assumptions of their existence. The gospel of love would not always be received lovingly by those whose existence was based on fear and greed. There would be, as Matthew's hearers had already experienced, many false messiahs who would try to temper or dilute the Gospel and suggest there was another way. And, indeed, there would be times when wickedness seemed to feed upon taking advantage of those who chose to live without protecting themselves in the vulnerable love (agape) that Jesus suggested was characteristic of the new age. At such times it would be natural for such love to grow cold or for people to become cynical and bitter about the response they were receiving.

Pain is not always negative. Sometimes it is the necessary prelude to something new and good.

Painful experiences were the necessary labor pains for new birth. The one who endured the labor pains would experience the new life, and it was this very new life which would become the witness to the world of the kingdom. It is only by passing through such experiences that the end would come. The Parousia was not to be something that God imposed on the world through a supernatural force that decimated the enemy while the faithful watched in safe isolation. Rather, it was to be something that God drew out of the world by means of the labor pains of the faithful. The fullness of the kingdom was a gift, but the gift was realized only by those willing to pass through the labor pains of birth. Matthew's message is one of endurance in the face of opposition, and inviting the faithful to examine the pain of the opposition for signs of God's fruitful presence.

Faith in the Wise and the Foolish

We need to pay attention to both the wise and the foolish in the faith. It is in the lives of the foolish that we experience the full power of God's grace.

In the parable of the wise and the foolish maidens, 25:1-13, Matthew warned against the self-righteous temptation of believing that because one has passed through some of these labor pains that she or he has gained insight superior to others. The normal interpretation of this parable must be challenged because it seems to imply that the selfishness of the wise maidens, when they discovered the plight of the foolish maidens, was acceptable. The normal interpretation, which you can find in almost any commentary, would suggest this to be an eschatological parable or a story of the final culmination of history. The bridegroom is seen as Christ and the bridesmaids as people of faith who await the second coming of Christ. The delay of the parousia, or the second coming of Christ, finds half the maidens unprepared and running out of oil. The wise do not feel they have enough to share and send the first set off to buy their own; but upon returning, the door has been shut and the bridegroom refuses them entrance. Understood in that manner, the parable urges preparedness and reinforces the lifestyle of those who already "have" and who feel justified in keeping what they have for themselves.

In the thirteenth chapter of Matthew, in which many parables of the kingdom are related, what the kingdom is compared to is always seen as a reflection of God or the word of God. In this parable the kingdom of heaven is compared to all ten maidens, which would correspond to the mustard seed (13:31) or the leaven (13:33). Seen in this light, the word of God, in the form of the ten maidens, goes out to meet the bridegroom.

Because of the power of the image of Jesus as the bridegroom in Matthew 9:15, and the suggestion in Revelation that the church is the bride of the lamb (Revelation 21:9), it is automatically assumed that Jesus was to be seen as the bridegroom in this parable as well. But this interpretation then allows the parable to fly in the face of grace and makes salvation something earned by preparedness that can be selfishly protected in the face of the need of others. However, if we free ourselves from that assumption, the parable takes on new meaning.

Consider people as the bridegroom and the maidens as the bearers of the word of God. The word of God is expressed both in those who are wise and those who are foolish. New disciples come to be married or to celebrate the new relationship with God in the presence of those who bear the word of God. Many of Matthew's hearers would be more comfortable in the presence of the "haves" than in the presence of the "have nots." After all, the "haves" have shown wisdom in planning ahead and, for Matthew's urban congregation, as well as most of ours, such wisdom is culturally comfortable. But if these new disciples receive the word of God only from the well prepared but selfish maidens, they have to accept a certain selfish nature that colors their understanding as well.

The word of God is also carried by the foolish, who could all too easily be dismissed as deserving their condition because of their lack of pragmatic wisdom. Yet if the kingdom of heaven is to be compared to all ten maidens (25:1), then by denying access to the five foolish, such disciples may be ignoring the impact of grace which tempers the temptation to selfishness that all too often comes to those who have been introduced to the faith. Responsibility is important. Without it, grace can be cheapened. Yet it is only half the container that bears the word of God to the wedding party of faith. People must always be alert, because no one knows either the day or the hour that

> RESPONSIBILITY IS IMPORTANT. WITHOUT IT, GRACE CAN BE CHEAPENED. YET IT IS ONLY HALF THE CONTAINER THAT BEARS THE WORD OF GOD TO THE WEDDING PARTY OF FAITH.

God's word may speak to them, and it would be a tragedy if at that time they responded "truly I tell you, I do not know you."

The True Disciple

The danger of a prosperous church or Christian is that we can miss the signs of the kingdom because they seem to threaten the benefits we enjoy.

The contrast between the old world and its ways versus God's new creation in Christ is described in 26:6-13. The incident took place in the home of Simon, the leper. Leprosy was a fearful disease that caused one to be shunned by the community. Simon was considered an outcast, yet Jesus was sitting at the table with him. Whether by presence or healing touch, Jesus has restored Simon to communion. In Jesus presence, there are no outcasts in the kingdom.

Next came a woman to anoint Jesus with a jar of very expensive perfume. This act ties together two very special events. People were anointed before burial in order to consecrate them to God, and kings were anointed in recognition that they were selected by God to serve the people. The latter was done first by prophets (I Kings 19:16) and later became the exclusive privilege of priests. But here something new was beginning. It was God's new creation, which Jeremiah had predicted, where "a woman encompasses a man" (Jeremiah 31:22). This unnamed woman, like the prophet-priest Samuel so many years before (I Samuel 16:13), inaugurated the new kingdom, which in another contrast with the old world began in death and apparent defeat.

Jesus' own disciples saw her extravagant act as a failure to be faithful to the commandment to be charitable to the poor (Deuteronomy 15:7-8). The law actually declared that if the people would obey God's commandments, there would be no poor in the land (Deuteronomy 15:4-5). But Jesus recognized that until all people obeyed God, until the kingdom of God was acknowledged by all people, the opportunity for people to practice their faith through sharing with the poor would continue (Deuteronomy 15:11). What the woman had done was to recognize that unique moment in time that inaugurated the new kingdom, even though, as in the case of David, there would be considerable passage of time before he was fully acknowledged (1 Samuel 16:1-13).

The "beautiful thing" which the woman had done was to prepare Jesus for death by acknowledging him as king. Later, her act would be affirmed by God when Jesus triumphed over death in the resurrection, but by her act, she anticipated and pointed to what God would do. By her demonstration of love, faith, courage, initiative, and self-sacrifice, she epitomized the true disciple in the new kingdom.

For Matthew the fact that a woman perceived what the male disciples could not was just one more piece of evidence of the shattering of the old structures in order to make room for the new. Matthew's congregation, if composed of the upwardly mobile merchant class who were often shut out of the aristocracy of the agrarian elite, would hear good news in both the sign of the leper being restored and the shattering of the possessive hold of the male inner circle.

> A WOMAN PERCEIVED WHAT THE MALE DISCIPLES COULD NOT

It was also a radical reminder that the kingdom of God could be recognized only if one were willing to prepare for the death of the old. Like the disciples, being a follower of Jesus does not necessarily guarantee that a person is prepared to make that response. Wherever the gospel of Christ is preached, each person and each church must hear the story of this lady's actions and be prepared to give up the old if they are to receive God's future even now breaking in on them.

Matthew reinforced in 27:19 this theme of a woman's insight into what the men in power were unable to see when he made reference to Pilate's wife sending a message to Pilate. Whereas Pilate could see in

Jesus only a political problem, his wife said, "Have nothing to do with that innocent man, for today I have suffered a great deal because of a dream about him." Again, we see the freedom that God displays in the number of channels through which the divine truth can be revealed. Also we are again reminded that when those who have been granted authority are unable or unwilling to perceive the truth before them, God often will speak through those who are kept powerless by the structures of society. The fact that Pilate's wife was a pagan forcibly reminds us that possession of faith is no guarantee that God will choose us as a channel of revelation.

Collapse of the Old Creation

Are we still fighting the battles of the old creation because we have failed to recognize and respond to the new creation in our midst?

The context of 27:55-56, with the women still present at the cross, demonstrated the collapse of the *old creation* and old way and the beginning of the *new creation* and new way. Jesus had breathed his last. The result was a new immediacy of God in the world, signaled by the tearing of the curtain that had previously separated the people from the "holy of holies" in the Temple. In the *new creation*, life reigns over death (27:52-53), and the Gentile centurion and executioners recognized Jesus as the Son of God. The gospel is universal and breaks the bonds of the past life/death bonds, Jew/Gentile bonds, and in these verses, the bonds of tradition with respect to men and women.

For if the Jews had been ethnocentric and needed the gospel to reveal the universal nature of God's word, even more would they have been locked into their patriarchal culture. Matthew hinted at overcoming the male-female division in the opening genealogy in which women, even foreign and questionably moral women, provided

> THE FIRST PERSON MENTIONED IN THE GOSPEL WAS MARY, AND THE FIRST PERSON IN THE NEW CREATION WOULD ALSO BE MARY.

the vital link. Also, the first person mentioned in the Gospel was Mary, and the first person in the new creation would also be Mary.

In the first four prophecies that Matthew saw fulfilled by Jesus, the first spoke of a woman bearing the word of God (1:23), and the next three made use of images of the feminine side of God. In the middle of the Gospel, the tension between the insular gospel and the universal gospel was exploded by a foreign woman (15:21-28). As the world neared the breaking point of the old creation, the only one who was able to perform the true role of prophet and priest in recognizing Jesus and anointing him for reign in the kingdom of God was a woman (26:6-13). All of these events culminated in the beginning of the *new creation* in which mention is made of the women who have ministered to and followed Jesus from the beginning and, unlike Israel (represented by the twelve disciples) did not abandon, deny, or betray him.

Some of these same women were the first to whom the risen Jesus appeared. As with the true priestess (26:6-13) and symbolic of the responsibility of the new creation to the old, it was these women who carried the message to the disciples. The new creation carried the word to the old Israel that it too might be reconciled in Galilee to the one Word of God. This Galilee, as referenced in 4:15, is the Galilee of the Gentiles, the place where Jew and Gentile mingle. Three of the women who were prominent in Jesus' life were specifically mentioned, though, unlike Mark, Matthew only mentioned by name those called Mary. While it is made clear that there were many women besides those named Mary, it is as if Matthew were saying it began and ended with Mary.

By failing to be specific about any behavioral change brought about by the new creation, the suggestion was being made that the new creation was *conceived*, but there was a time period before it would come to birth. Or, does it depend not so much on the chronological passage of time as it does on our response to the reality of the new creation before us?

CHAPTER 4

RESPONSE TO A WORLD DIVIDED INTO WEALTHY AND POOR

Our pursuit of security can become a barrier to our faith journey.

Though Matthew's Gospel began with a genealogy that normally would be of interest mainly to the wealthy aristocracy who, as has been mentioned previously, were trying to defend the purity of their bloodline, there were enough anomalies within the list to alert the reader that there was something new or different about this family tree. Then, as a child, Jesus was visited by the Magi who offered him gifts of gold, frankincense, and myrrh. As has been mentioned previously, those Magi had gained their wealth through offering their wisdom and advice to rulers. Then they subordinated their wealth to the child Jesus. For Matthew's urban merchants, whose security in life could not be maintained by bloodline but who were protected by their gathered wealth, the challenge to submit that wealth to the service of Jesus would be immense.

Necessary Preparation

We have to prepare ourselves to get beyond our dependence on wealth for security.

In 3:1-12 Matthew introduced John the Baptist, who stood within the framework of the Old Testament prophets. His message made clear that one must repent or turn from that which one had depended on for security within this world if one were going to be prepared to receive the new thing that God was doing. John quoted from Isaiah 40:3 that spoke of the necessity of people making preparation in order to receive God. Matthew had already made clear that, though Jesus was born into this world, Herod and all Jerusalem, including the chief priests and scribes, missed the significance of what God was doing (2:2-12). If such politically and religiously educated people could miss what God was doing, the issue of being prepared was not an idle one. The economic implications of John's call for repentance as preparation for receiving God was hinted at in the resistance to John's preaching indicated in 11:7ff. Luke made this economic challenge explicit (Luke 3:10-14).

As has been mentioned previously, the first temptation (4:3-4) was clearly economic.. As the Son of God, the temptation was not only to manipulate the gift of divine favor into self-controlled security, but also to display one's divinity by becoming the source of bread for the world. For many in Matthew's congregation, whose wealth had been the source of their security and status, the temptation to maintain their dependence on wealth for their security under the guise of retaining the resources to help the hungry would be very real.

Forming a Christian Community

We need to belong to a community that helps break down the barriers.

Upon beginning his ministry, one of the first things Jesus did was form a community. In the calling of the first four disciples (4:18-22),

Matthew gave the first glimpse of this new community that would represent the kingdom. Peter and Andrew were seen by Jesus "casting a net into the sea," which may suggest that they were economically poor as they had to fish from the shore. In contrast, the second set of brothers, James and John, were apparently on a boat owned by their father that had more than one net. The

> THE KINGDOM WOULD BE MADE UP OF BOTH RICH AND POOR, AND THE POOR WOULD BE THE FIRST CALLED. THE FOUNDATION OF THE KINGDOM WOULD BE A COMMUNITY THAT RECONCILED THAT WHICH NORMALLY DIVIDED PEOPLE.

kingdom would be made up of rich and poor, and the poor would be the first called. The foundation of the kingdom would be a community that reconciled that which normally divided people.

It is also important to note that their call took place not in a religious setting or even when they were at leisure but in the midst of their profession. There is a play on words captured in English in the RSV. "...They were fishermen. And he said to them, 'Follow me, and I will make you fishers of men.'" This passage may suggest that the issue was not the choice of occupation, but of allowing Jesus' call to transform the objective of one's profession and life from personal success or profit into serving and enhancing the lives of people. They could still fish, but the objective of their fishing, and indeed the objective of all professions, was (is) the enhancement of life for other people.

As Jesus identified with people at baptism and refused to manipulate people by their needs, overwhelm people by his power, or even control people by his position (4:1-11), so he called a community around him whose focus in life also would be other people. Neither the differences in wealth nor previous family, economic, or professional commitments must hinder their response to be servants of others.

For people whose life included substantial involvement in the economic structures of life, Matthew's Gospel meant a call to let Jesus' vision of the kingdom completely transform the use of their possessions on behalf of others. In an agrarian economy in which wealth was often a significant factor in dividing class from class, the fact that Jesus' community began with a dissolving of that economic division formed a significant challenge to Matthew's church.

Facing Economic Divisions

We live in a world in which the gap between the "haves" and the "have-nots" continues to widen. The burden of overcoming that division rests on those who have been blessed with more than others.

In the Sermon on the Mount, Jesus began to probe the vision behind the sixth commandment, "You shall not murder" (5:21). He declared the essence of the Law and the Prophets was not fulfilled just by avoiding the physical act of killing but must include every aspect of that relationship. To be continually angry with, to abuse, or to demean another violated that relationship as surely as if one took deliberate physical actions to cause that person harm. He further declared that an act of faithfulness to another person was an act of praise to God. In fact a failure to be reconciled in one's relationships with others made a mockery of any acts of worship. If we were ready to offer our gift, Jesus said, and then remembered someone had

> ONE CANNOT OBEY THE SIXTH COMMANDMENT AND IGNORE THE ECONOMIC INEQUITIES WITHIN OUR WORLD.

something against us, how could we expect God to value our worship until we had demonstrated the value of that other person by first trying to be reconciled (5:23-24)? For the Christian community to ignore the anger of the poor within our world created by the disparity between the wealthy and the poor would be to make a mockery of our worship of God. One cannot obey the sixth commandment and ignore the economic inequities within our world.

Matthew's Gospel was adamant that Christians be pursuers of such reconciliation. Speaking to people familiar with the world of commerce,

Matthew made clear that such reconciliation included economics by quoting Jesus in terms that would be familiar to people involved in commerce, "come to terms quickly with your accuser." If you have borrowed money, you had better be on good terms with the one from whom you have borrowed. Otherwise, if the note should come due and you are unable to pay, your creditor will have no mercy (5:25-26). In the Lord's Prayer, Matthew continues the emphasis on economics by suggesting that our debt with God would be directly related to our clearing up our debts in relationship with others (6:12). Though such a use of debts included all areas of life, it clearly did not exclude the area of economics. We are to be peacemakers, not just by eliminating conflict but by eliminating the causes, the feelings, the justifications for conflict. It is not a question of who is right and who is wrong in an area of conflict. The burden is on us who have been dignified by God to so dignify others that they would have no reason or feeling of ought against us. Healthy relationships with other human beings are essential to our worship of God. With all the inequities and resentment over economic disparities in the world, who could possibly find their worship of God as acceptable? Only those who offer their strivings for reconciliation with others as their gift to God, and then recognize that even their worship is received as an act of grace.

The Seduction of the Material

Sharing what we have with the less fortunate is healthy only when we do it as an act of worship.

One of the three acts of piety that Jesus commented upon in chapter 6 was that of the giving of alms. Alms giving was a recognition of one's blessedness--people who have received should also freely give. Alms giving was also a reflection of striving after righteousness. If a people were faithful, there would be no poor (Deuteronomy 15:44ff) because the Lord would bless the land; and there would be enough for all. So the giving of alms to the poor was both a striving after righteousness and an act of faith in God's faithfulness. But that act of piety could easily be distorted into a self-serving act when a display was made of it.

For most people, the first difficulty is to recognize that everything we have is a gift. This recognition loosens our grip on what we have so that we are free to give. It is no longer a possession to protect but a gift to be used. The second difficulty is seeing the act of giving as having its own intrinsic value so that we are not caught up in the debate as to whether we are being misused or abused by the receiver. If the value of giving is dependent on the response of the one who receives the gift, then giving is no longer an act of piety, i.e., worship of God, but rather a negotiation with another person for praise. To give alms free from any dependence on response is to give as an act of worship. The purpose of such giving is an uncalculated way to pray in action rather than words. It is to say in behavior "Your kingdom come, your will be done" because you recognize both that all of life is a gift and that in a world faithful to God's will there will be no one in want.

In 6:19-21 Jesus focuses on the seductive relationship we can have with the material in our lives. "Do not store up for yourselves treasures on earth, where moth and rust consume and where thieves break in and steal,...For where your treasure is, there your heart will be also." By focusing our attention on the gathering together of the material, as if it would protect us for the future, we focus our attention on death rather than life. Instead of seeing animals, nature, and people as friends contributing to the fulfillment of life, as it was in the Garden of Eden, we suddenly sense each (symbolized as moths, rust, and thieves) as potential enemies that threaten us. When we live against death, rather than for life, we assume the position of God, the giver of life, rather than our position as the ones who live life.

Jesus' teaching was focused on breaking the syndrome of sin, that suspicious nature which alienates us from all around us. We can do that only if our treasure, the focus of our hope, is in heaven or beyond the same fear of death that drives the rest of the world. Life begins in promise, full of potential. Heaven is the biblical symbol of the fulfillment of that promise. Jesus taught that our hope lay in the Fulfiller of Promises who could not be defeated by death in any of its forms. Yet, it is difficult to shift our focus from the material to the spiritual, from that which proves so vulnerable to that whose promise is eternal. Jesus taught that where our treasure is—that which we value as the true source of our hope—there our hearts, the seat of our commitments and decision making, would be also. We have to decide whether our hope lies in the giver or the gift.

> WE HAVE TO DECIDE WHETHER OUR HOPE LIES IN THE GIFT, OR THE GIVER

"No one can serve two masters..." (6:24). When we reflect on the loyalties and perceptions which shape our lives, we are finally faced with the truth of the choice before us. Our lives cannot be devoted to both the spiritual (God) and the material (wealth). One or the other must be our Lord. Our Lord is that person, thing, or belief that gives direction to our lives. We have to decide upon what we depend for our freedom from want, our happiness, our security, and our final hope of salvation. What are we willing to compromise, ignore, or sacrifice in the face of real want? The other is our Lord.

Though both the spiritual and the material are part of our lives, Jesus made clear that people could not choose money as the source of their security, gathered at the expense of time and energy focused on the spiritual dimension of their lives, and then hope that God would come through for them when, in the end, money could no longer fulfill its promise. We must clearly decide whether the material or the spiritual can offer us fullness of life, then regularly act in ways that make clear which is the servant and which is the Lord.

God is the ultimate vision of the spiritual, but the spiritual is experienced in love, justice, truth, purity, beauty, and graciousness as they reflect God (Philippians 4:8). We first begin to understand which is our Lord when we observe whether we are willing to compromise or risk the material on behalf of the spiritual or vice versa. Money, possessions, health, and life itself can either become gifts or our master. We choose. Life in the kingdom is not imposed upon us, but is a matter of free choice. It is only by repenting, or turning from the false loyalties, that we can recognize how close at hand the kingdom is.

An Age of Anxiety

It is ironical that we often make material goods the focus of life; and yet with all the food, clothing, and drink worries resolved, life can still be very empty.

In 6:25-33 Jesus began to explore what life was all about. The material aspects that cause people so much anxiety--what they shall eat, drink, and wear--Jesus saw as hollow trappings rather than the essence of life.

Jesus poked fun at people's undue anxiety about the future by contrasting it with the almost carefree attitude of the birds who survived from day to day. Then he suggested that undue anxiety was a reflection of how people devalue themselves in the eyes of God. God has given humans a gift of the ability to plan for the future. This is a gift not given to birds. "They neither sow, nor reap, nor gather into barns." Such a gift reflects the value with which God holds us. Yet people have taken the humanizing gift of a sense of time, which allows them to reflect on the past and anticipate the future, and allow it to be captured by the destructive spirit of anxiety. Jesus pointedly asked whether the spirit of anxiety that people allowed to dominate their lives could in fact alter the length of their lives.

Again Jesus poked fun at people's concern for clothes by contrasting Solomon (symbol of wealth earned by wisdom and planning) with the simple lily of the field. Jesus saw the spirit of anxiety as the destructive product of materialism. The Gentiles, those who had no awareness of a loving God, focused their lives on such things. But for Jesus, the essence of life, that which filled life with meaning, went far beyond the material. If, suggested Jesus, we focused on nurturing our relationship with God and pursuing God's righteousness or justice, those material things would be seen in the proper perspective of being a blessing that we have received.

Anxiety, as opposed to foresight, is an undue worry about something that has not yet happened. Tomorrow we cannot control. We can do only whatever we can today and trust that God will be with us regardless of what tomorrow brings.

Among the urban merchants of Matthew's congregation, whose status and security depended upon their ability to gather enough wealth that the upper class would have to give them respect, Matthew quoted Jesus in 6:34 as saying, "So do not worry about tomorrow, for tomorrow will bring worries of its own. Today's trouble is enough for today." Matthew's age, like ours, was an age of anxiety. Jesus also poked fun at how people let the spirit of anxiety dominate them, when in fact by anxiety they could not alter in the least what might happen. He adjured people to expend their energy resolving the problems of the day, which they could affect, rather than wasting their energy on tomorrow, which they could not affect. It was not a judgment on planning, which they can do today for tomorrow, but rather a judgment on anxiety--that expenditure of energy on worry about controlling what people were not able to control.

The truth is that we do become anxious about future events--worrying about whether we will complete the necessary preparations, meet people's expectations, et cetera. Like materialism, such anxiety is focused totally on a product:: Will the result be that people will like me? Will the result be a good sermon? Will the result be a successful meeting? Materialism can only survive on the product. Such anxiety is lessened and we are set free to do whatever we can but not be unduly anxious when we recognize the spiritual dimension of reality. Such a dimension gives us a worth not dependent on the product or the response of the world around us and allows us to draw on a renewable strength in the process so that we always gain.

Responding to a Gracious Word

If people truly open themselves to God, they can trust God to receive their every request with love and respond to it in a way that enables them to grow in their love for God and others.

In the Sermon on the Mount, we were warned against false piety, the perils of materialism, the destructiveness of anxiety, and the danger of judging others or, the opposite, of trivializing the holy so that we have nothing unique to offer. But in 7:7-12 Matthew assured his congregation that God was not a negative God but rather a God of promise. "Ask, and it will be given to you..." If you truly ask, seek, and knock, it will be given to you; you will find; it will be opened for you.

There is a twin edge to this promise. As many have discovered, to a limited extent, it is built into the universe that single minded persistence pays off. But it is also true that such persistence carries with it the built in judgment of the narrowness of the pursuit. Matthew's congregation had, in many cases, succeeded in gaining wealth by their seeking after it. They were discovering, also, that such wealth and success could be at the cost of all that was valuable in life.

The more hopeful part of the promise was that God is like a good parent who will respond in the best interest of the child. God would neither give stones for bread, nor would God give a serpent (harmful fish) just because someone asked for a fish.

Even selfish or short sighted requests will be received in love by God who will then stir our hearts to new insights. God sees the hunger that prompts even a selfish request and responds to the hunger if we will but receive it. Because of this, we are set at liberty to respond to others as we would want them to respond to us. "In everything do to others as you would have them do to you;..." The more we are sure of God's loving care for us, the more we are set free to respond to others in a loving manner. We love because God first loved us.

Our freedom to choose our response is an essential part of the relationship.

Jesus taught that one must "Enter through the narrow gate; for the gate is wide and the road is leads to destruction..." (7:13). Later, Jesus would be quoted in 22:14 as saying, "For many are called, but few are chosen." All people are called to the fullness of life, but few are chosen because few

> "FOR MANY ARE CALLED, BUT FEW ARE CHOSEN." ALL PEOPLE ARE CALLED TO THE FULLNESS OF LIFE, BUT FEW ARE CHOSEN BECAUSE FEW CHOOSE TO RESPOND TO THE CALL.

choose to respond to the call. Still, what type of response is called for? With such sterling examples as Jacob and David before us, it is clear that the narrow way is not primarily concerned with morality. Even Jesus, by the standards of the day, was considered of questionable morality-- he broke the Sabbath, associated with sinners, was accused of being a drunkard and a glutton, et cetera. So what is the narrow and what is the broad way?

The book of Deuteronomy emphasized that though the material world was part of God's good creation, its very blessings could still become a temptation to forget that God was the source of all goodness (Deuteronomy 8:17-18). The two ways that one could choose to respond to the promise of the world were called the blessing and the curse (Deuteronomy 11:26-29), or the way of life and death (Jeremiah 21:8-9). Jesus described this choice as the narrow and the wide gate. Jesus had previously distinguished between the material and the spiritual view of life and had promised that God would give good things to those who asked God.

The broad way is the material way. It has the appeal of our being in charge. Whether it is the way of wealth, pious formulas, or the latest psychology, we are continually tempted to build up our own security. Jesus suggested that the attempt to control the future would be filled with anxiety (6:25-33) and leads to destruction.

The narrow way appears less appealing because we have much less control. It is trusting that there is power beyond both sight and present appearance that can fill our spirit with strength. Like David, our reception of that strength does not depend on our morality, which we control by our own decisions, but on our trust in a power we cannot control. It was that trust that Matthew recorded Jesus exhibiting in 27:50 when he yielded up his spirit on the cross.

A congregation, like an individual, feels a stronger temptation to trust in its own capacity to gain control, than to trust in God who gave it life.

Therefore, for both the congregation and the individual, the way is hard that leads to life, and those who find it are few. Even the narrow way has its own temptation to turn our trust into a charade of irresponsibility, such as"Let God pay my bills." To really trust God is scary because there are no formulas; but it means being set free to life.

Finding the Center

We all want to feel we have built our life on a solid foundation.

Jesus concluded the Sermon on the Mount with a parable about a "... wise man who built his house on rock..." (7:24-27). The rock or the firm foundation for Jesus was recognizing the subtle temptation that comes to us in "sheep's clothing" to tempt us off the path of life. For Jesus, life is discovered through recognizing the choice of centering our lives on the will of God that is discovered in right relationships.

Such a life would not be free of conflict and adversity--the rain, the flood, and the wind came upon both the foolish and the wise in the parable. Just as the sun shines on the evil and the good (5:45), so the storm is experienced by both. The issue becomes not whether we will experience the same as the next person, but whether our lives are centered on an experience of faith in One that transcends the experiences of life and is faithful to us in both the good and the bad.

To be centered in that way requires us both to hear what Jesus said to us and to respond by actions in our own lives. In concluding this sermon, Jesus claimed an absolute authority to his words and that in him we could discover a center that would not prove unfaithful to us when our life was threatened. He was suggesting, also, that the natural adversity in life was such that without the foundation rock, life would eventually discover its own limitations and would fall. The rock is discovered in relationships with others and is not a secret we can discover and possess. But in both hearing and doing the words, we discover a faithfulness to us that transcends all that we might encounter in life and death.

Economics and Compassion

We are always tempted to want to fit our compassion into the framework of our perception of economic reality.

In the story of the healing of the two demoniacs in 8:28-34, Matthew confronted the issue of the Christian response to the tension between compassion and economics. When Jesus and his disciples had arrived by boat at the country of the Gadarenes, they were met by two demoniacs. This couple was so possessed that they were no longer in control of themselves and lived among the tombs of the dead. Though they were frightening, the community had learned to live with their presence among the tombs.

The demons within the couple immediately recognized Jesus as the Son of God, "Have you come here to torment us before the time?" The word used for time is *kairos*. It suggests not chronological time but rather a divinely appointed moment. The faithful believed that there would come an eschatological moment in history when God would utterly defeat evil and goodness would triumph. If that time of final judgment had not yet come, what was the role of ministry in the meantime? Jesus, confronting the demons before that final moment, suggested that God's future was already breaking in on the present moment and that the task of ministry was to give signs of that new reality by defeating the demons that were in opposition to God's rule wherever they met them.

There is an economic reality to facing fully the demonic forces that are distorting God's future even as it enters the present. "Now a large herd of swine was feeding at some distance from them," a clear indication that this was Gentile territory, as Jews would have nothing to do with pigs. The herd of swine also indicated the economic structure of the village as their most likely market would be the Roman military occupation troops. As the story would indicate, a village could tolerate and incorporate the demon-possessed couple much more than it could risk a threat to its economic structure.

Because it was before the time of final judgment, evil in the form of the demons was not just eliminated. God does not eliminate evil by violence. The demons still had the freedom to pursue their own destructive path. Given that reality, Jesus, in combating evil, preferred to risk harm to pigs rather than people, so he sent the demons into the pigs. The crazed pigs then ran down a hillside, fell over a cliff, and drowned in the waters below. Since the watery depths were considered the home of the demonic, they were returned to their place of origin. When Jesus placed a higher value on the healing of the two demoniacs than he did on the immediate economic structure of the "large herd of swine," the village came around and asked him to leave.

There is a sense in which there is always an interrelationship between those who hurt in a community and the economic structure of that community.

The demons of violence that possessed the couple were seen by the community to present an issue of law and order and of how to protect the greater community. The problem was solved as long as the couple was confined to the tombs (jail). If the demons were cast out, the issue would then become one of justice for the dispossessed couple that would call for a reallocation of funds and an upsetting of the economic structure of the village. The cost to the community's economic possessions in restoring the couple was greater than they wanted to pay. Jesus had a different view of the priorities in ministry.

Economics and Ministry

Ministry takes place in the midst of the economic realities of the world.

In reporting on Jesus' instruction to the twelve before they were sent out on a mission, Matthew illustrated the interplay of economics on ministry (10:5-15). In carrying our their mission, they were to demonstrate the true character of Israel. This special calling of God, together with the divine gifts to carry it out, was not to be bartered in return for special favors from those who benefit from their ministry. "You received without payment, give without payment." The ability to offer this healing ministry was a free gift from God and should be shared freely. There may be an implied criticism here of the religious leadership who were profiting from their positions at the expense of the people. This would certainly be consistent with Ezekiel 34:2ff in which the prophet denounced the religious leadership for profiting off the people.

At the same time, the Christian message was clearly relational and, therefore, the proclaimer should not be totally independent of the community to which s/he ministers. Ministry is not a one way street. Even as you minister to a community, the community should minister to you. "Take no gold, nor silver, nor copper in your belts." By coming needy into the community, without gold, silver, copper, two tunics, et cetera, the disciples provided the community an opportunity to minister to their needs even as they were ministering to the needs of the community. There was no suggestion that the one coming into the community should be kept at a poverty level, "for laborers deserve their food," but religious leaders should not become rich in the process either. For Matthew's people, and for us, there would be the strong suggestion that those who try to minister to others

> THOSE WHO TRY TO MINISTER TO OTHERS WITHOUT ALLOWING THEMSELVES TO BE VULNERABLE ENOUGH TO RECEIVE MINISTRY AT THE SAME TIME FAIL TO RECOGNIZE THE RELATIONAL CHARACTER OF THE GOSPEL

without allowing themselves to be vulnerable enough to receive ministry at the same time fail to recognize the relational character of the gospel.

The question of the extent to which one could expect the community of faith to respond to the material concerns of the world was addressed by Matthew as he described the event of Jesus feeding the five thousand in 14:13-23. Jesus had been teaching this large crowd in a lonely place throughout the day. As the day drew to a close, the disciples (the church) became concerned about the overwhelming need of the crowd for food. They urged Jesus to send the crowd away to fend for themselves but Jesus responded that they did not need to go away and that the disciples could give them something to eat. The disciples (the church), seeing the vast need of the crowd (the world), said that their resources were too meager to respond to such a huge need. "We have nothing here but five loaves and two fish."

From a practical viewpoint, the response of the disciples was quite correct. Their resources, in relation to the need, was quite inadequate. Jesus told them to give what they had to him and to tell the crowd (the world) to sit down (to prepare to be fed by the church). Then Jesus blessed the food and gave it back to the disciples (the church) to give to the crowd (world). When the disciples risked giving what they had in response to the world's need, they discovered that, by the blessing of Christ, what appeared to be meager from a practical viewpoint had become ample to meet the (world's) need and then some.

Jesus increasingly drew the disciples into active participation in mission. It was they, not Jesus, who actually fed the crowd. So for Matthew's people (and us), they could not expect the hunger of the world to be fed without their being willing to risk sharing what they had, in the context of Christ's blessing, with the world. The promise of God, of which Jesus' action became a living parable, was that if they (we) were faithful to God and shared with those in need, there would be no poor (Deuteronomy 15:4-11). Yet, in the meantime, they (we) needed to share what they had received.

The Inner Transformation

True freedom in life can only be discovered by placing one's complete trust in the giver of life.

The economic barrier by which one is shielded from access to God is emphasized by the story of the rich young man who came to Jesus seeking eternal life (19:16-22). Matthew, unlike Mark and Luke, avoided the disclaimer by Jesus that he should not be addressed as good because only God is good. Instead, the focus is on "what is good" and is resolved by Jesus pointing to "who is good," (19:17). This passage may well be Matthew's means of emphasizing the shift from deed to relationship. One does not do a deed or complete a task for which one gains eternal life as a reward. Rather, one relates to others in a manner that reflects the one "who is good" and thereby begins to experience the full, rich quality of the messianic age.

This emphasis was continued as Jesus responded to the man's question by quoting from the commandments and choosing those commandments that concentrated on people's relationship with each other. In Matthew, Jesus follows Exodus 20:12-26 more closely than in the other Gospels. Lest there be any doubt as to the thrust of Jesus' remarks, he added the saying from Leviticus 19:18, "You shall love your neighbor as yourself." To truly love your neighbor as yourself you must be willing to be as vulnerable to your neighbor (defined in Luke as anyone in need, Luke 10:29-37) as to yourself.

The young man immediately revealed the ability to practice the outward form of such commandments while still protecting oneself. He said that he had practiced these commandments, but still sensed a lack in his life. He thus exhibited a problem that has plagued the Church from its beginning. He was able to practice the outward form of faith while not allowing such practices to result in a transformation of the person. Jesus addressed the central issue by telling him that if he wished to experience fulfillment in life (the word translated "perfect" has the sense of maturity or fulfillment), he would have to divest himself of that which gave him security. It had been made clear by several of the prophets that only when one placed full trust in God, rather than in an element of creation like wealth, could one experience a true relationship with God (Habakkuk 2:4). In this instance Jesus, following the prophets, told him to sell all that he had, to divest himself of all security other than the security of God's faithfulness.

It was this radical dependence on God that the young man was unwilling to risk; therefore, he had blocked the inner-transformation for which he yearned. It was that final letting go of the alternative route to salvation in case God did not work out, that the young man, and most Christians since, was

> IT IS THAT FINAL LETTING GO OF THE ALTERNATIVE ROUTE TO SALVATION IN CASE GOD DOES NOT WORK OUT, THAT THE MOST CHRISTIANS ARE NOT ABLE TO MAKE.

not able to make. This emphasis on vulnerability is consistent with the preceding unit of 19:13-15, in which Jesus described vulnerable children as characteristic of those who discover God's future. Like children who are trustingly dependent on their parents, so Christians must learn to rely on God. Matthew's urban congregation would understand this concrete illustration of the subtle ways in which we think we are being faithful and yet are hedging our bets with other ways to secure ourselves against the uncertain future. This continued the central theme of Matthew's

Gospel that, like Jesus, his followers could discover the true freedom of life only by placing their full confidence in the Giver of Life. To do that, one must discover the God-like experience of being vulnerable to another. In our culture, where financial security is emphasized often at the expense of relationships, we can feel the full tension of Jesus' challenge to the young man. Only in the poorer economic strata, where security is dependent on relationships, do we begin to discover people who live out the truth of Jesus' message. It may be that we can receive such truth only by becoming vulnerable like the poor.

Contrast of World Views

How do we discover how to trust in the power of God's saving love in our lives?

When Jesus suggested that "... it will be hard for a rich person to enter the kingdom of heaven..." (19:23) and "... it is easier for a camel to go through the eye of a needle than for a rich man to enter the kingdom of God" (19:24), he was not making a categorical condemnation of wealth. Though the prophets clearly condemn those who became wealthy at the expense of the poor (Amos 5:11), rich people did become disciples of Jesus. Examples of rich people who became Jesus' disciples were Matthew (9:9), Joseph of Arimathea (27:57), and Zacchaeus (Luke 19:9). What Jesus was pointing out was the contrast between the way people normally think about life and the way of faith that enables one to experience the presence of God.

The disciples' astonishment, and surely the astonishment of Matthew's urban merchant congregation, was reflected in their questions. "Then who can be saved?" This permits Jesus to contrast the two world views. When one places trust in the normal forms of security and signs of success, the possibility of what Jesus spoke about seems utterly ridiculous. But the essence of faith that can provide one with the freedom to become truly human is not based on the wisdom of the world. As the traditions of Israel maintained from the beginning of their covenant tradition, it is God, not human wisdom, that ultimately proves faithful. When human wisdom dictated that Sarah was past childbearing age and that, therefore, the promise of God to provide Sarah and Abraham with children was impossible, God proved faithful (Genesis 18:9-14). Even more dramatically, when Israel had been defeated and all signs of nationhood were about to be wiped out, when there were no outward signs of security, Jeremiah affirmed that God was still the source of final trust (Jeremiah 32:17).

The danger of riches is that it provides one with a false sense of security and slowly seduces one into risking faithfulness to God rather than risking the security provided by wealth that originally was seen as a blessing from God. It is only when one recognizes that God can be trusted beyond the visible signs of security and success that one is able to let go of such signs, be vulnerable and, therefore, truly human to each other. It is then that one experiences God's reformed future that is already breaking in on our present. Jesus, by trusting God's faithfulness, was able to risk even his physical life and, thereby, shattered the pretense of death to rule over us.

The Reward of Faithfulness

What is the cost of faithfulness in our world?

But Peter, undoubtedly reflecting the questions of Matthew's urban congregation and our questions as well, said, "Look, we have left everything and followed you. What then will we have?" (19:27). Since Jesus' own life reflected that becoming vulnerable did not shield one from harm, nor always generate a warm response from others, what was the consequence of pursuing this path of faithfulness?

Jesus responded, "Truly I say to you, at the renewal of all things, when the Son of Man is seated on the throne of his glory, you who have followed me will also sit on twelve thrones, judging the twelve tribes of Israel" (19:28). It was a familiar theme in prophetic literature that all would be called to account for their behavior and that Israel would be the instrument by which God would judge the world (Obadiah 1:18). Being the instrument of God's judgment for the purpose of the world's salvation did not suggest, however, that Israel itself would escape judgment. The day in which God would regenerate God's vision for the world via new birth was often referred to as "The Day of the Lord" in the Hebrew Scriptures. In Matthew, it is called the "renewal of all things" when the truly human one, who became vulnerable on behalf of the vulnerable, is affirmed by the Creator. On that day, those who risk all security in faithfulness to Jesus' way, will become the criteria by which Israel itself is judged. All those who truly have become vulnerable on behalf of the weak and have exposed themselves as God has exposed God's self will discover that they have encountered the truth of what makes life eternal.

The sense of judging carries at least three connotations in the Old Testament that might be applicable. In the judicial sense, judging meant to decide in a dispute between two parties as to who was right and who was wrong. In this case the two parties would be those who have guided Israel in one direction and Jesus, who was disputing that direction. Jesus declared

> IF A JUDGE IS TO BE A DELIVERER, THEN, IN LIGHT OF THE CHRISTIAN HISTORY OF ANTI-SEMITISM AND PERSECUTION, CHRISTIANS HAVE CLEARLY FAILED IN APPROPRIATELY JUDGING ISRAEL.

that his followers would be able to settle that dispute. The second connotation was to deliver from injustice and oppression, as the judges did before there were kings in Israel. If a judge is to be a deliverer, then, in light of the Christian history of anti-Semitism and persecution, Christians have clearly failed in appropriately judging Israel. The third connotation, the one most often assumed in this passage, was that of ruling over. There is a sense in which those who have been vulnerable to the helpless would be in a position to administrate the ideal Israelite state.

The tendency towards triumphalism must be modified by remembering Jesus' constant admonition that such leadership for Christians must be in the form of servanthood (20:20-28).

In the new world, which was even then being created by the presence of Jesus, the consequence of the wealthy relinquishing the natural security of their wealth and instead becoming vulnerable was that God would use their witness as a testimony to the new way. The form of deliverance from oppression for the world would be rulers who first came to serve. This type of radical act would require an inner transformation of one's view of the world and the source of the things in it.

The Uncomfortable Kingdom

Faithfulness to God can challenge our sense of fairness measured by material possessions.

This transformed view was suggested by the parable of the laborers in the vineyard that Matthew records in 20:1-16. In an agrarian society, such as Israel in Jesus' time, much of the inherited land had been lost through years of rent, taxes, and high interest loans. Instead of each household or extended family having a sufficient plot of land to assure its livelihood as was originally intended and protected by Israelite law (Leviticus 25:23-28), many of the people had become essentially landless. This meant that their only means of livelihood was hiring out to the large land holders who often took advantage of their need, squeezing out maximum work for minimum pay. But the kingdom of heaven, the reformed future that God had in mind, was just the opposite in focus. There the true owner of the land, which is always God (Leviticus 25:23), was mainly interested in the land producing that which was necessary for livelihood. Therefore, the landowner in Jesus' parable hired laborers for the denarius, which in Jesus' time was the usual day's wage.

When, later in the day, the landowner found others standing idle in the market place—wanting to be hired but finding no one to hire them–he told them to go to work and "I will pay you whatever is right." Jesus' hearers would have assumed that one more landowner was able to take advantage of one more desperate peasant to get much work for little pay. The process was repeated three more times, the last occurring at the final hour of the day. In this last instance, it was emphasized that the laborers' lack of work was not due to laziness but due to lack of opportunity, "Because no one has hired us" (20:7).

Now came the surprise. This landowner was somehow different. He did not seek to squeeze the maximum work for the minimum wage. When those who worked only one hour came for their pay, they received a full day's wage. Their families would not be desperate on this day but be able to eat a decent meal. As God had promised, when Israel is faithful, there will be no poor (Deuteronomy 15:4f).

But there was a second surprise in God's kingdom. When those who worked a full day came for their wages, they expected the stratification of society to hold and they would get much more. Like the elder brother in the prodigal son, they were furious when the one-hour workers had their livelihood restored to them and they, who worked all day, received only what was agreed upon. God's promise was that the land would produce enough but they wanted to get wealthy from the land. God reminded the hearers that the land was God's and God was not obligated by people's efforts to give them special rewards. "Or are you envious because I am generous?" The workers were begrudging the owner's (God's) compassion on the less fortunate without any recognition that their full day's work was also an act of compassion. Each day in the new world was to be a day of gratitude for what one had received, including the opportunity to work and produce. When the landowner said, "Take what belongs to you, and go...," the workers were forced to realize that what they had that belonged to them was very little, and so it is with us.

Choosing Priorities

The real issue becomes that of deciding what is most important in life and recognizing the consequences of that decision.

This is made clear in the parable of the wedding feast as recorded in 22:1-10. Imperial control in an agrarian society was secured by the allegiance of petty city states to the imperium. In such a system, the loyalty of the city state was given only begrudgingly, and when there was any reason to believe that the king's control was weakening, there would be rebellions or, at the very least, a refusal to give the tribute and signs of respect that the king demanded. For a king to give a marriage feast for his son would be to have arranged for an alliance by marriage with another kingdom in order to secure his power. He would then invite those city states over whom he held sway to come to the wedding feast to give recognition to the newly formed alliance. The fact that the king in the parable issued two invitations to those who owed him allegiance and they both refused to come and mistreated his servants would indicate that they believed his power was weak enough that they could successfully break away from his rule. The king reacted in fury and sent his troops to assert his dominion by destroying the rebels and their city. The fact that it was a city which was destroyed indicates that the king responded to political entities and not individual guests.

But then the parable takes its surprising twist. Up until now the listeners would have been familiar with the endless power games of the ruling elite and one more attempt to shift the balance of power that failed. But now the king tells the servants to go out into the thoroughfares and invite anyone that can be found because those originally invited were not worthy. To suggest that those which would be found in the streets, "both good and bad" were more worthy than even

TO SUGGEST THAT GOD'S KINGDOM MIGHT REJECT THE UPPER CLASS, REGARDLESS OF THEIR BEHAVIOR, IN FAVOR OF THE RIFFRAFF THAT EVERYONE KNEW WERE UNCLEAN AND UNWORTHY, WAS REVOLUTIONARY.

the rebellious members of the ruling elite was without precedent. To suggest that God's kingdom might reject the upper class, regardless of their behavior, in favor of the riffraff that everyone knew were unclean and unworthy, was revolutionary. This parable might well remind the listeners of the first time when God was looking for a people, yet overlooked the established nations and chose to form a people out of an eclectic group of slaves and rejects from society.

The new alliance, sealed by the wedding feast, was one between God and those who responded to the invitation without excuses of property considerations (farm) or economic consequences (business). Of course, one might argue that the riffraff did not have such positions or possessions to risk, but that viewpoint reinforces Matthew's point of how such things can subtly insert themselves between people and God's invitation.

While God is extraordinarily gracious to everyone, our own response to such grace can effect how we experience the fullness of life.

Lest one think that this parable is simply about choosing sides against the wealthy, Matthew adds an ending unique to this Gospel (22:11-14). The king, who had sent his servants out to the thoroughfares to invite "everyone you find," came in to look at his guests, upon spotting one without a wedding garment, he had the man ejected from the wedding feast.

Though the invitation had been thrown wide open, the banquet was not to be attended without proper respect for the host. It was not the quality of the wedding garment, but the lack of one that offended the king. Even a poor peasant would have had some type of wedding garment. To come without such a garment would have indicated that he came for the food or what he could get out of it, not to share in the celebration of the event.

The parable suggests that the fullness of life is offered to all those who will respond to the invitation regardless of previous status and possessions. However, one's response to such a gracious invitation could become a hindrance. People who entered as aggrandizers, whose only focus was on what they could get for themselves, could not hope to remain to experience the fullness of the gift. The partial psalm quoted as the guest was ejected, "...where there will be weeping and gnashing of teeth,'" was Psalm 112, which spoke of righteous people as those who distribute freely and give to the poor. Those were the signs of a person who recognized that what he had was a gift rather than a right. The closing phrase, "For many are called, but few are chosen," emphasized that one's response to God's gracious invitation was crucial to experiencing the fruits of that invitation and, therefore, would direct Matthew's hearers (and perhaps us) to reflect on their (our) generosity or lack of it in response to the needs of others.

CHAPTER 5

TENSION BETWEEN TWO CREATIONS

Signs That Challenge Our Doubts

What do we look for when we begin to have doubts?

John the Baptist sat in prison and heard about the ministry of Jesus. From

prophecies like Malachi 3:18, in which the prophet spoke of the coming of the Messiah as a time when "...once more you shall see the difference between the righteous and the wicked, between one who serves God and one who does not serve him," John expected the Messiah to usher in the great eschatological or final judgment that would separate the wheat from the chaff (Matthew 3:11-12). In contrast to these expectations, what John was hearing from prison was that Jesus associated with all sorts of sinners and broke laws like those pertaining to the Sabbath, so John began to have doubts as to whether Jesus was indeed the Christ. He sent some of his disciples to find out(Matthew 11:2-3).

Jesus' response was, "Go and tell John what you hear and see: the blind receive their sight, the lame walk, the lepers are cleansed, the deaf hear, the dead are raised, and the poor have good news brought to them" (11:4-6). Because Jesus' ministry forced people to make choices, one result was division (10:34-39); however, the focus of his ministry was a restoration of *shalom* to God's creation. His healing activity fulfilled such prophecies as Isaiah 29:18-19, 35:5-6, and 61:1. Through Jesus' presence, all of creation was being healed and restored to God's original intention. It was because of these activities that the message that Jesus was the Christ could be carried to John.

Part of Christ's continuing ministry was to communicate to the world that it is not locked into a continuing cycle of despair.

Matthew's people were often overwhelmed by the negative and filled with questions of doubt like those John asked. To counter such doubts, Matthew quotes Jesus as declaring that there were signs of shalom and healing interrupting the despair and breaking into people's lives all the time. These were moments of grace that loosened the soil for the planting of the seed. Like John, these experiences of shalom and healing disrupt the logic of people's cynicism and respond to their personal questions as to whether the Christ has come.

The ministry of the church is both to name the name of Christ in the world and to continue the ministry of shalom.

Matthew reminded his urban congregation that like the Hebrew children leaving Egypt (Exodus 13:21-22) and the twelve disciples in the time of Jesus, the glory of God goes before them. They have been given instructions in the Scriptures to know what signs to look for and how to interpret the shalom of wholeness toward which these signs point. The healing work of God happens outside the church as well as within, but the church has been given the responsibility of telling the story that can interpret that which is everywhere manifest.

The Threat of the New Creation

People who believe only in their own power and want to remake the world according to their own designs will resist strongly the counter reality of Christ. The task of the church is not to please those in power, or be universally loved, but to be faithful to the one who first loved us.

> THE HEALING WORK OF GOD HAPPENS OUTSIDE THE CHURCH AS WELL AS WITHIN, BUT THE CHURCH HAS BEEN GIVEN THE RESPONSIBILITY OF TELLING THE STORY THAT CAN INTERPRET THAT WHICH IS EVERYWHERE MANIFEST.

Having responded to the questions of John's disciples, in 11:7-15 Jesus turned to the crowd to talk about John the Baptist. Matthew was aware that many people had rejected Jesus' message and were undoubtedly rejecting its proclamation by Matthew's congregation as well. The reason for this rejection, Matthew suggested, was their inability to accept John's message of repentance that prepared the way for hearing Jesus' proclamation of the kingdom.

The reason they could not accept John's message was that they, like most people, wanted their faith domesticated so that it served them, rather than offering new responsibilities in light of their faith. When people heard what the prophet John was saying, they flocked to hear him. Then they complained because John did not mold to their needs (a reed shaken by the wind), nor did he take account of society's etiquette (one dressed in soft raiment). The role of the prophet was to challenge people in a way that prepared them to receive God's news.

Jesus identified John's ministry by a quote that seems to be from Malachi 3:1 and gives allusions to Exodus 23:20f. The context of the Exodus passage was a set of laws concerning justice and the promise of an angel who would go before the Israelites. If they would be obedient to this angel (Exodus 23:21), the result would be a healthy and prosperous life. The Malachi passage also dealt with a messenger who confronted the issue of injustice (Malachi 3:5). The message was that if people would not confront the injustice in their lives, the coming of God would be unbearable; but if they did repent of their complicity and began to live according to God's laws of justice and equity, the results would be a healthy and prosperous life (Malachi 3:10-11). By these references, Jesus reminded people of the economic and social justice issues of John's call to repentance (Luke 3:7-20), which Jesus declared had to be faced before one could experience the full benefits of shalom which Jesus was offering.

The fact that John boldly confronted those issues in society, and, thereby, prepared for the coming of the Lord as prophesied by Malachi, made him one of the great figures of humanity. But, because in the kingdom that Jesus proclaimed there was no such hierarchy, the least in the kingdom would be greater than John (11:11).

In 11:12-15 Jesus talked about the violence which had associated itself with the advent of the kingdom. Those who had felt judged by John's and Jesus' confrontations had reacted violently, and such events as the arrest of John (11:2) were attempts by people who lived by violence to control the in-breaking of this new reality. For Matthew's people, who lived after the destruction of Jerusalem and the Temple, John's imprisonment was also a clear example of people of violence, the Romans, trying to remake the kingdom in their own image.

Christians were thus warned not to mistake the absence of conflict for the presence of the kingdom. "...The kingdom of heaven has suffered violence, and the violent take it by force" (11:12). Whether a bold prophet or a simple believer challenged the state, the presence of one who was absolutely faithful was a radical challenge and a threat to the world as it was. People who believe only in their own power, and want to remake the world by force, will often react with anger and violence to such a challenge as was raised first by John, then by Jesus, and later by the continuing Christian community.

The violent story of Ahab and Jezebel's response to being confronted by Elijah (1 Kings 18:1-19:3) was only unique in that it was so graphic. The violence was a typical response to God's message when people such as Elijah brought it to those in power. If John was Elijah returned, people should not have been surprised that the response was similar.

> IF BEING A FAITHFUL WITNESS CAUSED SUCH A VIOLENT RESPONSE IN BOTH THE OLD AND THE NEW TESTAMENT, CAN THE CHURCH EXPECT ANY LESS?

If being a faithful witness generated such violent response in both the Old and the New Testament, then the church should expect that there would continue to be such response. They are forewarned not to dismiss those who proclaim the gospel to the needy because the response of those in power is that of violence.

Raising the Level of Tension

To accept Christ as Lord is to challenge those who seek to claim our loyalty to their vision of the world.

The tension between the old creation and the new creation mounted in 21:1-11 as Jesus neared Jerusalem. Jesus appeared deliberately to stage his entrance from the Mount of Olives, which would evoke the Messianic image of Zechariah. The Jews saw their occupation by the Romans, as they had other humiliations in the past, as a reflection of the judgment of God on the Day of the Lord (Zechariah 14:1-3), but they also believed that such judgment was for the purpose of salvation and not just to vindicate some pristine sense of divine justice (Zechariah 13:1). When a time of judgment was completed, when it had served its purpose, then God would complete the final purpose of all divine judgment and effect salvation. God would turn and be an advocate for God's people (Zechariah 14:3). That moment would begin at the Mount of Olives and end with God being recognized as sovereign over all the earth (Zechariah 14:9).

Evoking that image, Jesus sent two disciples to secure "a donkey tied, and a colt with her." Matthew, unlike Mark and Luke, apparently misunderstood the poetic parallelism and thought the quote from Zechariah 9:9 referred to two animals. The image was Messianic: God's king, unlike the Roman counterparts of whom the crowd was accustomed, was "humble, and mounted on a donkey..." This king recognized that God was the true sovereign, and the king was a representative charged with executing justice on behalf of the people.

Like the coronation march of royalty, the people prepared a way for the "people's Messiah." Lest there be any doubt, Matthew combined the Zechariah quote with Isaiah 62:11b. The setting for the Isaiah passage was the preparation of the "way for the people." Perhaps Matthew deliberately misunderstood Zechariah's quote to allow for "one" to ride beside the king in order to remind the king of the limits of Messianic sovereignty or to combine the two figures of Zechariah.

In any case, the crowds caught the symbolism and shouted, "Hosanna to the Son of David!" Hosanna means *save us*. The Davidic covenant suggested that God's salvation would come out of the line of David. In the city of Jerusalem, ruled by the Romans and already made tense by the Passover celebration of hope for Jewish freedom, Jesus' entrance drew a clear contrast between those who presently ruled and the God who came to effect justice. This could easily apply both to the Romans and the Jewish leaders who had made accommodation with them. No wonder the people stirred and questioned the identity of this one who was willing to exacerbate the tension within the city.

The crowd still identified him as a prophet from the backward province of Galilee. Eschatological hope, when it impinged upon the accommodation that had been made with the world as it was, raised the tension between what was and what would be to the breaking point. To wistfully hope that God would *save us*, Hosanna, was different from being willing to face the disruption that such salvation brought to the accommodation that had been made with the world. As Matthew's hearers knew, many people both suffered and benefited from the unjust structures of the world. It was easier for the crowd to bracket Jesus as a prophet from a remote province than to face the full implications of his presence.

Choosing Between two Realities

We face a conundrum of divided loyalties.

Jesus' manner of entering Jerusalem as God's conquering representative (Zechariah 9:9); his cleansing of the temple (21:12-13), which suggested it was corrupt beyond human reform (Zechariah 5:5-11); his identification with the expendables instead of the priests and scribes (21:14-16 and Zechariah 10:3-5); and his symbolic judgment of the fig tree (21:18-19 and Jeremiah 8:13), which was indicative of a legitimate expectation by God of these leaders (Micah 7:1), all raised the question of authority. Within an agrarian society, it was the priests who were charged with judging right and wrong. They were the legitimizers of society and the ones who, by their position, were deemed to be closest to God.

Now the legitimation of the legitimizers was being challenged. They disputed Jesus' right to do this (21:23-27), and Jesus, in a proper rabbinic manner, answered the priests' question with a question. Was the authority by which John baptized for repentance from heaven or merely human convention (21:25)? In Matthew's account, John also had challenged the Pharisees and the Sadducees, and suggested that they were like a fruitless tree (3:10 and Jeremiah 11:16). Within Israelite society, the one who was allowed to challenge the given order of things was the prophet, provided he spoke what God told him to speak (Deuteronomy 18:20). If the chief priests and the elders affirmed that the source of John's call for repentance was from God, then Jesus could legitimately ask them for the signs or fruit of their repentance which would have the effect of confirming his own challenge to them. But, if they disavowed John, they would be rejecting a figure whom the people held to be a prophet. Because of the Israelite tradition that lent dignity to all people within the society, the religious leaders' own authority still rested to some degree on acceptance by the people and the belief that God would fight against leaders who failed to be faithful (Zechariah 10:3).

Jesus caught the priests in the conundrum of their divided loyalties. When they were unwilling to make the choice between loyalties, Jesus refused to answer their question as to the authority behind his actions. This passage may imply that the reason the chief priests and elders refused to answer Jesus question was that they really did know the answer to their own question, but refused to acknowledge it.

For Matthew's people the conundrum of divided loyalties in this world was captured in the dilemma of the religious ruling elite. Jesus' proclamation of the nearness of the kingdom challenged people to decide between the divine authority experienced in the presence of Jesus and their loyalty to the old understanding of reality. They were tempted by fear of the disruptive consequences on their life to not make that choice. Like the priests, they were tempted to avoid such a decision by raising the question of the authenticity of that choice. Jesus' response was not an assertion of divine power but, rather, a lifting up of the social consequences of people's choices on other people. He asked people to examine the fruit of their present life in light of what they already acknowledged was God's expectation.

Shaking the Foundations

The inequality of society needs to be challenged by people with power freely choosing to be servants of others.

In 23:1-12 Jesus took the offensive and posed a radical challenge to the religious leaders who had found accommodation with the present structures of the world. He affirmed the law which the scribes and

Pharisees interpreted, "(they) sit on Moses' seat; therefore, do whatever they teach you and follow it..." But, he accused these same religious leaders of not adhering to that very law. "...but do not do as they do, for they do not practice what they teach."

The implication, reinforced by his subsequent examples, was that the Law of Moses, or the structure of life that initially shaped a disparate group of people into Israel, was essentially an egalitarian structure without the heavy class stratification of their present society. In their current society, the ruling elite, of which the Pharisees were a part, disparaged manual work of all types and insisted that the lower class perform it for them. This distinction, which had no part in Moses' law, was apparent in Jesus' accusing the Pharisees of putting heavy burdens on people's shoulders but not lifting a finger to help. Status in the agrarian societies was displayed by very clear modes of dress. Religious symbols like phylacteries (Deuteronomy 6:8-9) and long, long tassels (Numbers 15:38-39) became a luxury that working people could not afford but were clear symbols of the elite class who did not work and had wealth. Places of honor at feasts, best seats in the synagogues, proper salutations in the market place, and being called *rabbi* by others were all prescribed ways that the lower-class people gave deference to their *betters*. In following such customs, the leaders were merely assuming the status that society assigned them.

Jesus saw such accommodation to class distinction, and all the benefits that accrued to the upper class, as a clear contradiction to that which was called for by the Law of Moses. No one was to assume the position of rabbi over others, because all were equal. To call someone *father* was a way of giving deference to someone who held status over another (2 Kings 5:13), but Jesus insisted that each was a child of God and, therefore, equal to the other. The same would be true, in

JESUS SAW SUCH ACCOMMODATION TO CLASS DISTINCTION, AND ALL THE BENEFITS THAT ACCRUED TO THE UPPER CLASS, AS A CLEAR CONTRADICTION TO THAT WHICH WAS CALLED FOR BY THE LAW OF MOSES.

reverse, of seeking to be called master. The disciples were neither to give status nor to claim status, but to relate to all people in line with the covenant expectation of justice and mercy.

The inequality of society needed to be challenged by people choosing to respond to the need of others by being their servants. This freely chosen action would demonstrate that they recognized that God intended to upset the unjust structure of society that placed some people in exalted classes above others. The rigidity of the class structure that Jesus was challenging may be hard for people to imagine who live in an industrial society that experiences a high degree of mobility. Every facet of dress, speech, and mannerism and the total structure of the society was designed to set the elite off from the lower classes. Jesus was shaking the very structure that held things together. The fact that he would have been heard gladly by the lower classes only served to make him a greater threat to the upper classes because, as a distinct minority, their power was maintained as much by lower class acquiescence as it was by any force the upper class brought to bear.

Funeral for an Old World

We need to grieve when the practices of our faith serve simply to reinforce the inequalities of our society.

In 23:13-36, Jesus offered a funeral lamentation for the scribes and Pharisees as if they and the world that they represented were already dead and the grieving process should begin. The word translated *woe* in Greek connotes sorrow and lamentation and corresponds to the Hebrew word that also is translated *woe* in the NRSV suggesting a funeral lamentation. These lamentations have a parallel in the six *woes* of Isaiah 5:8-23, or seven if you include the one in Isaiah 20:1-4, which may have been misplaced.

The first lamentation referred back to religious leaders' failure to practice what they preached (23:3). By their behavior, which conformed to the class stratification of their society (23:4-7), they neither participated in the possibilities of the kingdom, nor did they make it available to others. "…For you do not go in yourselves, and when others are gong in, you stop them" (23:13).

At this point some manuscripts add an additional woe, which reinforces the message by means of a concrete illustration: "Woe to you, scribes and Pharisees, hypocrites! For you devour widows' houses and for the sake of appearance you make long prayers; therefore, you will receive the greater condemnation" (23:14 NRSV footnote). The issue was one of justice that included special attention to the most vulnerable in society. From the beginning of Israel's life, the widow, the stranger, and the fatherless were singled out for special concern because they were the most vulnerable. It was easy for the wealthy, through lending practices or in this case, temple taxes, to place the vulnerable into such heavy debt that the rich were able to foreclose on what little the poor had. The fact that the priests participated in that stratified system was bad enough, but they compounded the problem by displaying pious devotion through offering long prayers on any excuse, but ignored the plight of the needy on every excuse.

With the breakup of the kingdom and the dispersion of Jews throughout the world, centers of Jewish faith in the form of synagogues were spread throughout the Gentile world. Because of the heavy emphasis on monotheism and high ethical standards, Judaism appealed to many Gentiles. Jesus recognized this situation in his third lament (23:15), which recognized the great physical efforts made to acquire new converts, but in the process of moving the adherents into full membership, the scribes and Pharisees, by their hypocritical behavior, distorted the very appeal that attracted the Gentile in the first place. The result was a cynical or disillusioned convert who was twice as far from the justice of God as were the Pharisees.

Though the urban merchants who heard Matthew recite these funeral orations may have delighted in hearing the pompous Pharisees upbraided by Jesus, they could not fail to hear the word of warning that underlay such stories. They lived in a highly stratified world, and the temptation was always to try to secure a grip on the next rung up the ladder or certainly not to upset

THEY LIVED IN A HIGHLY STRATIFIED WORLD, AND THE TEMPTATION WAS ALWAYS TO TRY TO SECURE A GRIP ON THE NEXT RUNG UP THE LADDER OR CERTAINLY NOT TO UPSET THE SYSTEM FROM WHICH THEY WERE BENEFICIARIES.

the system from which they were beneficiaries. In what way were they re-enacting the very features of distortion that they could so clearly see in the Pharisees?

In 23:16-22 Jesus pronounced a lament on the blindness of their approach to oaths. Apparently, scribal interpretation of the use of oaths held that swearing by the gold of the temple or the gift of the altar was more binding than swearing by the temple or the altar themselves. Drawing upon the Mosaic tradition, which traced back to God's instructions concerning the tent of meeting and its altar (Exodus 12:26-29), Jesus showed how the gold was made sacred by the temple and the gift by the altar. Then, stepping beyond casuistic law, he suggested that no oath could be given that does not involve the very sacredness of one's relationship with God. His logic was that it was God who had made sacred what was on the altar and had promised to be present in the temple and, indeed, filled the very heavens themselves; therefore, how can anyone swear by anything in the universe without referring to God? By the intricacy of such interpretation, the Scribes had guided themselves down a blind alley; so how could they hope to offer themselves as guides to others (15:14)? Since interpretation of the Law was the very reason for the scribes existence, Jesus' lament over the way in which the Law, which was meant to protect one's freedom, had become an oppressive burden was in fact a funeral lament over the scribes themselves. That which had been meant for life had been sapped of its vitality and had become a living death. For Matthew's people (and for us), the implication of the danger of creating too rigid a structure and set of church laws was clear.

Then, in 23:23-26, Jesus combined the theme of social justice and the practice of the ritual requirements of faith in order to lament how lifeless faith had become. The living death of the faith had not come about because they had refused to practice the faith, but because they had allowed the practice of faith to legitimize rather than challenge the injustice present in society.

In one sense, all religion lends legitimacy to society. Religion has a major function of bringing coherence to and making sense out of the experience of life. But in an agrarian community, the function of religion justified the stratified society in which the elite lived off the backs of the peasants and lower urban classes, because that was the way they believed God had ordained it.

Israel's faith also legitimated their society, but because the people's faith was based on a covenant with God who expected them to care for the poor and the vulnerable, the society that their faith legitimated was an alternative to the way the world around them lived. The laws of the covenant were designed to challenge the injustice of society. The tithe, for example, was intended as a reminder that all they had was a gift from God who called them to be a "light to the nations." But, Jesus lamented, the religious leadership focused on the tithe, even to the minute detail of such aromatic plants as dill and cumin, as if this was the fulfillment of the Law, rather than a pointer to the society toward which God called them. The religious leaders neglected the fuller vision that included "justice and mercy and faith" (23:23).

Such a separation of religious practice from life led to a ludicrous situation in which religious leaders appeared to be complete fools. In ribald humor, Jesus pictured the scribes and Pharisees as meticulously straining out gnats from a cup from which they were about to drink and swallowing a camel hump, hoofs, and all. To the crowd who was listening, this could not have elicited anything but loud guffaws.

Jesus pressed his point by adding a sixth funeral lament over the scribes and Pharisees who carefully cleansed the outside of the cup and plate but

> SUCH A SEPARATION OF RELIGIOUS PRACTICE FROM LIFE LED TO A LUDICROUS SITUATION IN WHICH RELIGIOUS LEADERS APPEARED TO BE COMPLETE FOOLS.

missed the extortion and rapacity within (25:25). The practice of religion was intended to aid in the transforming of society. The fact that one could comfortably participate in the practice of Israel's faith without any awareness of how this faith conflicts with the societal practices that rob people of their dignity and livelihood and that generate a sense of greed in people's character, was a judgment against those who would "cross sea and land to make a single convert" (23:15) and yet leave him or her untransformed in his or her daily life.

The Pharisees were supposed to be guides, but they were blind to the necessity of creating the vision of an alternate society in which the practices of faith were legitimating the proper vision of God's reformed future. By separating religious practice from daily life and God's purpose for that life, they had created a lifeless burden that oppressed rather than released people for a more human and, therefore, divine future.

Matthew's hearers could both rejoice in Jesus' challenge of Israelite leaders and hear the echo of a possible funeral lament for themselves as well if they (we) were not insistent on allowing the practice of their faith to support and legitimate God's vision of life. Their faith was to be a counter-pressure against all the forces that suggested that the inequities within society were just an inevitable part of people living together. For Matthew's community (and ours), there was an insistence on tying liturgy to life if our worship was to be full of life.

The final two laments in 23:27-32 made specific Jesus' declaration that the religious leaders had created a living death. It was part of Levitical law that contact with the dead made one ritually unclean and, therefore, barred one from access to communion with God (Leviticus 22:46 and Numbers 5:1-3). Therefore, on an annual basis, the tombs were given a coat of whitewash in order to make them stand out so that no one, especially the priests, would come upon them accidentally and defile themselves. An incidental result was that this practice beautified the tombs even as it covered up the dead bodies that the Israelites believed would defile them or make them unclean.

To recite a funeral lament over the scribes and Pharisees was much more radical than accusing them of being useless in what they did. To accuse them of being dead was to suggest that they were unclean and actually defiled people or made people unfit to commune with God. Though they might appear to be righteous, like the whitewashed tombs that were seen as beautiful, it was a cover for the defiling hypocrisy and inequity. The evidence of such hypocrisy was seen in the final lament in 23:29-36. Jesus pointed to the scribes and Pharisees who had accommodated themselves to the injustice of their society while they pretended to give great honor to the prophets who refused to make such compromises. The scribes and the Pharisees even had the gall to judge their ancestors for having killed the prophets, as if they were more righteous than their ancestors.

In retrospect, Matthew's hearers knew that those same scribes and Pharisees who were protesting their innocence would later take part in shedding the blood of Jesus, the prophet par excellence. This only added to the irony of their protestation. Their only hope was to confess and be open to the transformation of their lives. Short of such repentance, or turning around, their destiny was to fulfill the inherited traits of their ancestors.

The funeral lament, which Jesus recited over the scribes and Pharisees, became a radical challenge to any who would participate in the Jewish or Christian faith. The religious leaders had the vocation of providing the interpretation of the Law which gave guidelines for life in liturgy and celebrations, and enabled believers to participate in the drama of the faith. Jesus did not advocate the abolishing of such practices (23:3 and 23:23). Rather, he highlighted the deathly results of separating such practices from the weightier matters of justice and mercy within society. Such a separation of worship from life could contaminate or make unworthy a believer's approach to God and thus kill the very communion that the practice of faith was meant to generate and deepen the alienation that faith was meant to reconcile.

Death not in Vain

All acts of faith, no matter how seemingly ineffective in our world, will be used by God in the effecting of the divine purpose.

In order to emphasize that this was not just a debate of the past, Matthew quoted Jesus as saying, "Therefore I send you prophets, sages, and scribes, some of whom you will kill and crucify, and some you will flog in your synagogues and pursue from town to town..." (23:34). Originally the statement may have been a rough quote of 2 Chronicles 24:19 or 36:15-16, which referred to how God's compassion led to the continual sending of prophets to call for repentance. But Matthew knew the sending and the rejection of those who proclaimed the word of God did not stop with Jesus (10:17,23); therefore, he had Jesus speak the words about future situations that Matthew's people would face as well.

The effect of the final part of the statement "...that upon you may come all the righteous blood shed on earth, from the blood of righteous Abel to the blood of Zechariah the son of Barachiah... " (23:35) was that neither the first innocent death in the Bible, that of Abel in Genesis 4:8, nor the last death in the Hebrew Bible as it was arranged in the time of Jesus (2 Chronicles 24:20-22), nor by implication any death that had occurred by reason of one's faithfulness since that time had been in vain.

The "righteous blood shed on earth" (23:35) was because of the lack of a faithful response of those religious leaders who should have been guiding the world into a more faithful response. As with the prophet Hosea, Jesus placed a heavy responsibility on those called to be priests (Hosea 4:4-10). Such righteous blood should not be shed in vain but "will come upon this generation" (23:36). That is, the blood of the innocent shall mount up as a powerful and effective witness against the injustice of Jesus' time, Matthew's time, and each succeeding generation.

> GOD MADE USE OF THOSE WHO DIED IN FAITH TO BUILD A COUNTER-PRESSURE AGAINST THE FORCES OF INJUSTICE THAT DISTORTED THE VISION OF GOD'S FUTURE.

Again, death was not the victor or a means of defeating God's purpose. God made use of those who died in faith to build a counter-pressure against the forces of injustice that distorted the vision of God's future. The message to the scribes and Pharisees was that they had become a pollutant contaminating the world. The message to those who sometimes feel overwhelmed by the pressures against living faithfully in this world is that no act of faith can be killed by this world but God uses all such acts of faith to further God's purpose.

The Judgment Is Pronounced

When the practice of our faith seems empty, it may suggest that God has withdrawn until, by obedience, we can demonstrate our welcome of God's presence.

Because of the failure of leadership, Jesus proclaimed in 23:37-39 that the people, too, had experienced the consequences of the broken covenant (c.f. Hosea 4:9). Jerusalem, the holy city and the center of the nation, which should have symbolized justice and steadfast love, participated in the stoning and the killing of those who God sent to call them back to faithfulness. The voice of God's desire to protect both the people of God's choice (Psalms 36:7) and the place of divine residence (Isaiah 31:5) was now spoken by Jesus in the first person, "Jerusalem, Jerusalem, the city that kills the prophets and stones those who are sent to it! How often have I desired to gather your children together as a hen gathers her brood under her wings...." This exhortation suggested both a symbolic claim of divinity and the idea that the glory of God, the manifestation of God's presence, which was once symbolized by the Temple, now resided in Jesus. In the same manner that the prophet Ezekiel expressed the departure of the glory of God from Jerusalem (Ezekiel 11:22-24), Jesus suggested that the protective presence of God in him would depart Jerusalem as well. The question was left open as to whether God's glory would return from exile once again.

The whole series of laments from 23:13-37 were, in the liturgical form common in prophetic writing, known as the judgment speech. In a sense, it was like a prosecutor's summation in a trial that typically concluded with God pronouncing the judgment. The prophetic form of judgment, which would have been familiar to the religious leaders, drew upon the covenant formula expressed both in Leviticus 26 and Deuteronomy 28, in which obedience was to be followed by blessings and disobedience by curses. With the reading of the indictment, expressed in the series of funeral laments, the sentence followed in a form similar to Leviticus 26:31 and Ezekiel 12:20. "See, your house is left to you, desolate" (23:38). But more devastating than all, the covenant was broken and the glory of God departed: "For I tell you, you will not see me again until you say, 'Blessed is the one who comes in the name of the Lord...'" (23:39).

There is a double irony to this last statement because it is exactly what some of the crowd did shout upon Jesus' entry into Jerusalem; but the religious leaders would not receive him, so he, like the glory of God in Ezekiel 11:23, would leave Jerusalem and stand on the Mount of Olives. The message was clear. God's presence was not a guarantee that the leaders could manipulate for their own selfish gain. God's presence was part of a covenant that required a faithful response; and when such faithfulness was ignored, God's glory could depart and go elsewhere. God was not a magic amulet that could be manipulated for personal gain, but rather a God who invited a people into a relationship. Even as Israel experienced the absence of God in exile, so could Matthew's hearers (we) experience the absence of God if they were unwilling to respond to God's graciousness by living out the justice and mercy that God expects. God desires to offer the protective wing of her divine presence, but this is dependent on an obedient response.

Again, as throughout the Gospel, Matthew has Jesus use a feminine image for God at significant moments in his ministry. Here, Jesus used the image of a mother hen caring for her brood to represent God's love for Jerusalem.

Foreshadowing the New Creation

The communion service recognizes the presence of betrayal and alienation while at the same time offering signs of redemptive hope and reconciliation.

The final Passover meal, which Matthew described Jesus sharing with his

disciples (26:20-29), was traditionally a family meal. That Jesus ate it with his disciples was to suggest the intimate family-like character of the gathering. Further, to break bread with others was to enter into a covenant relationship with them. From the central covenant of the Exodus onward, such agreements were sealed with a meal (Exodus 24:11). The fact of the betrayal of Jesus was made worse because it came from within the inner circle, the intimate family of the faithful.

Matthew and Mark imply what Luke makes explicit: that Judas was present at the sharing of the bread and wine of the Last Supper. The first communion service was shared with a traitor whom Jesus had already acknowledged. Judas presence, together with his association with Judea, may be intended to make clear that Judas, and therefore

Judea, and in fact all of us who betray our vocation, can still feed on the bread of life and be restored to full community. In the new creation, which is foreshadowed in this meal, the bread of life and the hope of reconciliation are always present.

Jesus began by offering the traditional Jewish prayer of thanks. Then he broke the bread and gave it to his disciples. This would recall a similar process in 14:19 in which Jesus blessed the bread, broke it, and gave it to his disciples that they might feed all who were hungry. Only this time, Jesus commanded them to eat it as representative of partaking of his body, which also would be broken for them, and like the former incident, was to be shared with all those who hunger. The bread was symbolic of the blessings of God that the disciples were invited to share.

Then Jesus took the cup. The cup signified the destiny (20:22-23) of those who participated in this lifestyle of the new age. The cup of red wine also symbolized blood, which was the bearer of life. As Moses had done at Mount Sinai (Exodus 24:8), Jesus inaugurated the covenant with blood. As was true of the old sacrificial system, it was in the shedding of blood, the pouring out of life before God, that the past was canceled and a new hope was initiated.

Despite some manuscripts that add *new* to the covenant, this does not signify a break with Israel but a renewal of Israel. The traditional image of a vine for Israel was evoked here as Jesus utilized the symbol of the cup also to point forward to the anticipated messianic feast. The tension of betrayal continued to exist within the "Son of God" (Exodus 4:22). The full joy of the messianic banquet of God's intentions was still to be realized in the future, but its anticipation was foreshadowed in this banquet of the covenant initiated by the *son* who was in obedience to God. The fruit of the full vine would be drunk in the future when all of Israel was restored to full obedience.

THE COMMUNION SERVICE RECOGNIZED THE REALITY OF BETRAYAL AND ALIENATION WHILE OFFERING A PROLEPTIC SIGN OF HOPE.

The communion service recognized the reality of betrayal and alienation while offering a proleptic sign of hope. Later as the Body of Christ continued to share the bread, it gave thanks for and shared in the blessing of God discovered within the community of faith. When the Body of Christ drank of the cup, it shared in the destiny of this community which, for now, included the pain of brokenness and betrayal, but also included the sure anticipation of the messianic banquet. Here was a sign of the renewed and restored Israel at which the obedient son celebrates with the obedient children of Israel who have been released from all their oppression both external and internal. It will then be recognized that God transformed the evil of brokenness and betrayal into the means by which those who had been formerly outside of Israel (Gentiles) were included in, or grafted on to the one vine, Israel (Ephesians 2:13-16).

CHAPTER 6

THE UNITY OF THE PEOPLE OF GOD

Jesus as the Midrash on Israel

I want to propose that Matthew is proclaiming Jesus as God's Midrash of Israel's life as it is interpreted through the Scriptures.

The term Midrash is defined as the *exposition of the underlying significance of a biblical text*.[iii] My thesis is that Jesus embodied the life of Israel in his person and thereby revealed the truth of what God was accomplishing through the life of Israel.

Jesus took Peter, James, and John and led them up on a high mountain by themselves, and was transfigured before them. Here was revealed Jesus' true significance. Moses and Elijah appeared to them. The Law and the Prophets were conversing with Jesus. When Peter offered to provide hospitality for all three of them, "a bright cloud overshadowed them, and from the cloud a voice said, 'This is my Son, the Beloved; with him I am well pleased; listen to him!' When the disciples heard this, they fell to the ground and were overcome by fear. But Jesus came and touched them, saying, 'Get up and do not be afraid.' And when they looked up, they saw no one except Jesus himself alone" (17:1-8). For Matthew, Jesus was the Midrash, or interpretation of the Law (Moses) and the Prophets (Elijah).

What is the relationship between Christianity and Judaism?

Earlier, Jesus had tried to explain the necessary separation that was going to occur between his followers and Judaism. "Neither is new wine put into old wineskins; otherwise, the skins burst, and the wine is spilled, and the skins are destroyed; but new wine is put into fresh wineskins, and so both are preserved" (Mat 9:17). In essence, the faith of those who were to follow Christ was like green wine. Until Christianity had matured sufficiently, it could not fit within the structures that formed Judaism. As history has demonstrated, it was too aggressive and volatile to fit comfortably within Judaism. Originally Christianity did try to exist as a sect within Judaism but split within forty to sixty years.

Yet for Matthew, who wrote his gospel after the destruction of the Temple and the barring of Jews from the city of Jerusalem, it was important that the continuity of the one people of God be understood in all its fullness. God had not been defeated by Jewish obstinacy and forced to start again with a new "people of God." Jesus had not created a replacement for Israel, but rather embodied Israel in his own person so that believers could understand the truth of God's revelation.

This is a critical issue for the people of faith. If Israel's disobedience frustrated God's plan and caused God to break the divine promise made to them, then one would have to raise the question of whether the Church's disobedience would cause God to eventually give up on the church as well and try out yet another people or give up on humanity altogether?

Seeing the life of Israel in the person of Jesus.

Matthew pictures Jesus as answering the question of what would have happened to Israel in that politically volatile world if it had been strictly obedient to God in all that it did. Jesus was Israel fleshed out in one person. You can easily see the parallels between the life of Jesus and the life of Israel as reported by Matthew.

It began even before his birth. As had an earlier Joseph (Genesis 45:4-7), so now a new Joseph, also fathered by Jacob, became the protector of this embodied Israel (Matthew 2:13-15). Both Josephs had experienced betrayal, the first by his brothers and the second by his betrothed. Both were in a position of power that could have enabled them to exact retribution, but both responded with an understanding that God's purpose was not advanced by the exercise of vengeance (Genesis 50:15-21 and Matthew 1:18-25). As had happened at the beginning of Israel's lineage with Sarah's pregnancy (Genesis 21:1-3), so Jesus' birth was a miracle unexplainable by normal biological processes. As God would take a "no people" and make them God's people (1 Peter 2:10), so God formed Jesus in the womb of an unknown virgin teenager. As God called Israel his first born son (Exodus 4:22), so Jesus would be spoken of as God's firstborn son. In the same manner that the spirit of the Lord rested on David when he was anointed by Saul (1 Samuel 16:13), so the spirit rested on Jesus when he was baptized by John (Matthew 3:16). In the same manner that God led the people of Israel into the wilderness to test them and to cause them to understand that "one does not live by bread alone but by every word that comes from the mouth of the Lord" (Deuteronomy 8:2-3), Jesus was "led up into the wilderness to be tempted by the devil" (Matthew 4:1). The parallels continue as the story unfolds. As Moses went up on a high mountain to receive the Ten Commandments (Exodus 19:20), so Jesus went up on a high mountain to deliver the Sermon on the Mount (Matthew 5:1).

As Jesus continued his life, he demonstrated the interaction between God and Israel. The people of God could trust God in the midst of

> JESUS WAS ISRAEL FLESHED OUT IN ONE PERSON.

chaos. The God they believed in was able to still the chaos by speaking a word at creation (Genesis 1:3 ff), and, in a similar manner, Jesus was able to still the storm by speaking a word (Matthew 8:23). As Israel was able to cross the Red Sea (Exodus 14:1-29), so Jesus walked on water (Matthew 14:22-27). Yet, like the first Israel, so the Israel experienced in the twelve disciples were not always obedient. In the same manner that the children of Israel grumbled in the wilderness (Exodus 16:2-3), so Jesus' disciples often fought among themselves (Matthew 20:20-27). When the children of Israel were hungry in the wilderness, God fed them with manna (Exodus 16:4-5), and later Jesus would feed the hungry crowd in the wilderness (Matthew 15:32-38). As David, the anointed, refused to kill his enemy Saul (1 Samuel 24:1-22), so Jesus urged his listeners to "love your enemy" (Matthew 5:43).

As we move into the passion story, the parallels continue. As Joseph was betrayed by Judah for twenty pieces of silver (Genesis 37:25-28), Jesus was betrayed by Judas for thirty pieces of silver (Matthew 26:14-16). As Jacob, the father of the twelve tribes, wrestled

> AS JOSEPH WAS BETRAYED BY JUDAH FOR TWENTY PIECES OF SILVER JESUS WAS BETRAYED BY JUDAS FOR THIRTY PIECES OF SILVER

alone with God at the Jabbok River (Genesis 32:22-30), Jesus wrestled with God in Gethsemane (Matthew 26:36-46).

The issue throughout Jesus' entire journey was the same as that with which Israel was to be confronted in its journey. Both Israel and Jesus had to learn that God could be trusted in every circumstance. Abraham was asked to sacrifice his only son, the one possibility for God to fulfill his promise of progeny through Abraham and Sarah (Genesis 22:1-19), and God did sacrifice his only son, the only hope for the world (Matthew 27:32-54). While God prevented Abraham from carrying out the sacrifice, with Jesus, God raised him up to declare that God, not death, had the final word. The question was whether God would be faithful to God's promises. As God promised King David that his descendents would occupy the throne of Israel, so a child of the house and lineage of David became the king that sits at the right hand of God Almighty.

In Jesus we see the intention of God's call of Israel for the sake of the world.

Dawn of a New Creation

The new creation was one that was characterized by obedience to God and in which all barriers, or levels of status which might divide human from human, were removed.

"God saw everything that he had made, and indeed, it was very good. And there was evening and there was morning, the sixth day...And on the seventh day God finished the work that he had done, and he rested on the seventh day from all the work that he had done" (Genesis 1:31and 2:2). But toward what end had God created this world? We begin to see the answer in the eighth day of creation, or the first day of the new creation. "After the Sabbath, as the first day of the week was dawning,..." (Matthew 28:1).

We know from Genesis 2:2-3 that, during the first creation, God rested on the Sabbath. After Jesus' crucifixion, at the dawn of the first day after the Sabbath, a new creation is about to begin. The two Marys who maintained their vigil at the close of the old age, both during Jesus' crucifixion (27:55) and at his burial (27:61), are also the first to be present at the dawn of the new age (28:1). Matthew is clear that, in the same way that it was a woman who gave birth to the Word of God, it was women who refused to abandon Jesus at death and who were the first to greet him at the dawn of the new creation.

Again, as at the point of Jesus' death, so now there was an earthquake. If the first was in judgment that tore down the old reality (27:51), the second was in hope that opened up a new creation (28:2). The first destroyed the false separation between God and the people when the curtain separating the Holy of Holies from the common worshiper was torn in two (27:51). With the presence of God in the world, the grip which death held over the old world began to be broken (27:52). The second earthquake was interpreted as being caused by the descent of an angel (28:2). Biblically, an angel is the human manifestation of the divine or a messenger of God. The angel rolled back the stone and sat upon it, again demonstrating that where the divine presence is felt, death does not prevail.

As at the Transfiguration (17:2), the raiment of the holy was "white as snow" (28:3). An agent of revelation bridged the gap between the secular and the sacred. At the beginning of the Gospel, an angel appeared to the faithful in dreams, but now the sacred was so present in the world that the Gentile guards, as well as the Jewish women, recognized that something new had occurred. Nothing was said to the guards, but what they saw and experienced caused their understanding of reality to be shaken. When soldiers, who depended totally on the physical use of power in this world, encountered the divine, the very foundation upon which they had built their lives collapsed. They "became like dead men" (28:4).

On the other hand, those who came in faith had their fears calmed (28:5). Though frightened, they had come seeking, so the angel interpreted the meaning of the events they had experienced. "...I know that you are looking for Jesus... He is not here; for he has been raised...Come, see..." (28:5-6). These women were then commissioned to serve as bearers of this revelation to the disciples: "...Go quickly and tell his disciples, 'he has been raised from the dead,...'" (28:7).

The life of Israel in the new creation.

The new Israel, in the form of the twelve disciples, like the Old Israel, was huddled in fear. They needed the message of these two women to set them free. "Go quickly and tell his disciples..., and indeed he is going ahead of you to Galilee;..." This was the message by which Jesus had already prepared his disciples (26:32). This is the New Exodus and the New Creation. Jesus had been delivered from the bondage of death.

THE GOSPEL BEGINS WITH MARY WHO GAVE BIRTH TO THE WORD OF GOD AND IN THE END A NEW MESSAGE IS DELIVERED BY TWO NEW DISCIPLES NAMED MARY.

Like the Virgin Mary at the beginning of the Gospel who gave birth to the Word of God, a new message was delivered by two new disciples named Mary. A message of this new reality that had overcome the barrier of death was delivered by these women who had overcome the barrier of the sexes. They told the other disciples to meet Jesus at the point at which the barrier of nationalism was also overcome --Galilee of the Gentiles (4:15). Jesus was the center of a new beginning. The women responded with fear and joy, running from the tomb to obey the angel's command (28:8).

When these women responded in obedience to the revelation received, they met Jesus (28:9). So that there would be no misunderstanding, they heard him, saw him, and touched him (28:9). Jesus responded with essentially the same message as the angel. "Do not be afraid; go and tell my brothers to go to Galilee, there they will see me" (28:10). By their faithful response, the women already had met Jesus and were part of the new creation. The other disciples, being part of the old creation, must respond in faith by going to Galilee before they would meet Jesus and participate in the new creation.

Note one difference between the angel's message and that of Jesus: The angel refers to disciples or learners (28:7), and Jesus refers to siblings (28:10). For the first time in Matthew, Jesus indicated a horizontal relationship with the disciples. By joining him in the "Exodus" to Galilee, they joined him in the kingdom he had received. Thus, the question of who would sit with Jesus in his kingdom and who would have positions of authority, which was raised in 20:20-38, was now answered. In the new kingdom, which can only be entered through faithful obedience, there would be no need to compete for positions of status, because Jesus would relate to them as equals.

The Real Idolatry Exposed

The new creation has no room for the old forms of idolatry.

We know from 27:62-66 of the priests' desire to secure the tombs and of Pilate's insistence that the priests do so with soldiers from the Temple. The excuse given at the time was to prevent a fraud from being perpetrated, which given the religious charlatans in the world, seemed a reasonable precaution by people who bore the responsibility of guiding the faithful.

Then, in 28:4, we are told that the guards witnessed the angel and were overwhelmed by fear. And in 28:11 we are told that these frightened guards recovered enough to return to Jerusalem and report their experience to the chief priests. A quick meeting of the Sanhedrin was convened. If there was room for reasonable doubt as to the sincerity of the intentions of the religious leaders, now it was made clear. The chief priests and elders, confronted by evidence from an independent source, agreed to bribe the soldiers to conceal the truth from the people (28:12). The religious leaders who were responsible for spreading the truth of God to the people conspired with the soldiers of Rome to have a lie told: that the disciples stole the body while the soldiers slept.

The true emptiness of the opposition to Jesus was exposed. Up to this point, one could have excused it as honest doubt and skepticism. However, by the soldiers' testimony of their own experience and the Sanhedrin's choosing to respond with deliberate efforts to suppress what they now knew was true, the Sanhedrin were revealed as being in opposition to God. They denied the truth they had heard; they plotted to deceive the people; they compromised the integrity of the soldiers; and they undermined the authority of the governor by agreeing to use their influence to protect the soldiers if the governor learned of the soldiers' participation in the deception. To whom were the Sanhedrin loyal if not to God, or the people, or the reigning political power? The disciples may have abandoned Jesus in fear and confusion (26:56); Peter, in a moment of panic, may have denied Jesus (26:75); Judas, in weakness and confusion, may have betrayed Jesus (27:4); but the Sanhedrin plotted to suppress the truth because they felt it was more important to protect themselves than to respond to God.

> THE DISCIPLES MAY HAVE ABANDONED JESUS IN FEAR AND CONFUSION; PETER, IN A MOMENT OF PANIC, MAY HAVE DENIED JESUS; JUDAS, IN WEAKNESS AND CONFUSION, MAY HAVE BETRAYED JESUS; BUT THE SANHEDRIN PLOTTED TO SUPPRESS THE TRUTH BECAUSE THEY FELT IT WAS MORE IMPORTANT TO PROTECT THEMSELVES THAN TO RESPOND TO GOD.

Thus Matthew explained that the story spread among the Jewish people, that Jesus' body was stolen, was a direct result of the failure of the Jewish leaders to be loyal to the God of truth whom they represented. Their position as the religious leaders had provided them with enormous privileges of power and wealth among the elite. For the religious leaders to have responded to the truth proclaimed by Jesus, who had identified with the weak and helpless in society, would have meant they would have risked the benefits of their position. By choosing to protect their vested position, these leaders demonstrated that they were finally loyal only to themselves. They had become their own gods!

The Great Commission

The world is our parish.

In Matthew 28:16 the eleven, following the instructions given to them by the women, made their way to Galilee of the Gentiles (4:15). Unlike Luke and John, Matthew does not record an appearance of Jesus to the disciples in Jerusalem. As Jesus began his ministry (4:12-17), so he ended it in Galilee. So that there would be no doubt, for Matthew the Gospel began and ended where Jew and Gentile met. God's new creation was and is one of reconciliation, not separation.

The disciples who represented the new Israel were incomplete, only eleven, until they moved out into the world, where they would encounter the risen Christ who would complete their number. They went "to the mountain to which Jesus had directed them" (28:16). It was to the "mountain of the Lord, the house of the God of Jacob" (Isaiah 2:3), that these wrestlers with God (Israel) journeyed. As Isaiah made clear many years before, though the Law and the Word of God were first revealed in Zion, the Word must go forth from there because it had universal implications (Isaiah 2:2-4).

By following Jesus, the disciples were led out of Jerusalem and commissioned to teach God's ways to the nations of the world (28:19-20). For Matthew's hearers, who as merchants needed to associate with the pagans of the world, and for us, who live in a very mixed society, Matthew made clear that believers have an authentic commission. It is when the Law and the Word went out into the world that God would fulfill the divine intent that "...nation shall not lift up sword against nation, neither shall they learn war anymore" (Isaiah 2:4).

When the disciples saw Jesus, they worshiped him. Like the two Marys, they had no difficulty recognizing him. In contrast to the disciples behavior before the crucifixion, when they abandoned him, they worshiped him. The resurrected Christ was different from the human Jesus, but clearly recognizable. Yet, we are told that even as they worshiped him, "some doubted" (28:17). The doubts that existed in their minds did not prevent them from worshiping Jesus. Though Matthew clearly understood Jesus as having the capacity to perceive doubts and questions in people's minds (9:4), the doubts of some of the disciples did not prevent Jesus from receiving their worship.

We are not told about the nature of their doubts. Certainly to interpret and fully understand *what* they met was different from recognizing *who* they met. The nature or meaning of

> DOUBTS ARE ALLOWED TO REMAIN AS A GRATING EDGE TO KEEP US OPEN TO GOD'S FUTURE.

the resurrection was far more complex than merely seeing a person once believed dead. Was this a ghost or an illusion (14:26)? How does one respond to that which death cannot hold? Jesus did not find it necessary to resolve their doubts with rational explanations, nor did he feel a complete resolution of doubts was necessary before they could proceed. The disciples, and hopefully the Church, were not allowed to stagnate in self-satisfied complacency with all doubts resolved. Doubts are allowed to remain as a grating edge to keep us open to God's future.

Jesus' response to the disciples' doubts was to announce the beginning of a new reality. "All authority in heaven and on earth has been given to me" (28:18). The resolution of doubts was to be found in one's response to Jesus and not in rational explanations. Jesus was laying a claim to the fulfillment of Daniel 7:14 and, therefore, identifying himself explicitly with the "Son of Man." The mission that had been restricted to Israel during his earthly life (15:24) was now expanded to the whole world. Out of that authority, Jesus commissioned the disciples to share in this mission to the world. The new Israel, which was completed by Jesus who made twelve, was to break out of the old restrictions of confining themselves to the people of a particular religious tradition. The Church, if it is to be faithful to its Lord, cannot remain within itself but must accept its commission to minister to the world.

They were to make disciples of the nations, not just individuals (28:19). To be a faithful disciple of Christ was to accept the responsibility to introduce national structures as well as individuals to the teachings of Christ. To baptize nations in "the name of the Father and of the Son and of the Holy Spirit" was to bring them into a renewed relationship with God in all God's manifestations. The disciples' task was to be the means by which God restored the world to communion with the divine.

That process required teaching nations to observe what Jesus taught the disciples (28:20). This commission became Jesus' response to the disciples' doubts, both then and now. It was in obedience that their, and our, doubts would be resolved. Jesus did not remain behind as he sent them forth. As eleven ascended the mountain, twelve descended. "And remember, I am with you always" (28:20). These words echoed the great "I AM" who was present with Moses in the Exodus event (Exodus 3:12, 14), all the way through to fulfilling the prophecy spoken in Matthew 1:23–Emmanuel, God with us. As God was present when Israel first confronted the pharaoh and the political structures of the oppressive evil of slavery and began their journey to freedom, so now, as the disciples confronted the oppressive evil of the powerful structures of the world and the fears that distorted people's lives, God was with them.

God is in Christ reconciling the world to God and not counting our sins against us.

Matthew began with a genealogy which traced Jesus' origins to Abraham, who was commissioned to respond in obedience that all the families of the earth might bless themselves (Genesis 12:3). Matthew closes with Jesus' promise to be present with the disciples as they accept the commission to restore all the families of the earth to a true communion with God.

The task of the Church is both enormous and frightening. We truly wish to worship Jesus. Yet, when we look at the political structures of our world and the entrenched inequities within these structures, like Moses saw in Egypt in the first Exodus (Exodus 3:10ff) and the disciples saw at the edge of the new creation, we are filled with excuses and doubts (28:17). The only thing that makes it possible is Jesus' promise:

> "And remember, I am with you always..."
> (Exodus 3:12 and Matthew 28:20).

INDEX OF SCRIPTURE TEXTS

ENDNOTES

i   *The Origin and Destiny of Humanness,*Crystal Press, San Rafael, CA
    for Omega Books, 1976;*Herman C. Waetjen;* pages 28-31

ii

iii   Mirriam-Webster's collegiate Dictionary, Tenth Edition

www.ingramcontent.com/pod-product-compliance
Lightning Source LLC
Chambersburg PA
CBHW021637120626
46545CB00002B/591